Caring for Mother
A Daughter's Long Goodbye

Virginia Stem Owens

Westminster John Knox Press
LOUISVILLE • LONDON

© 2007 Virginia Stem Owens

Portions of this book appeared as the articles "What Shall We Do with Mother?" *Books and Culture,* March 2002; "Dances with Medicine Men," *Books and Culture,* April 2004; "In the Midst of Things," *Books and Culture,* September 2005; "The Visit," *Christianity Today,* September 28, 2004; "Thanksgiving at Fair Acres," *Christianity Today,* November 13, 2000; and "The Hour of Our Death," *Image,* Spring 2000.

Book design by Sharon Adams
Cover design by designpointinc.com

First edition
Published by Westminster John Knox Press
Louisville, Kentucky

PRINTED IN THE UNITED STATES OF AMERICA

07 08 09 10 11 12 13 14 15 16 — 10 9 8 7 6 5 4 3 2 1

Library of Congress Cataloging-in-Publication Data

Owens, Virginia Stem.
    Caring for mother : a daughter's long goodbye / Virginia Stem Owens.
        p. cm.
    ISBN 978-0-664-23152-1 (alk. paper)
        1. Owens, Virginia Stem. 2. Caregivers—Religious life. 3. Terminally ill parents—Care. 4. Parkinson's disease—Religious aspects—Christianity. 5. Adult children of aging parents—Religious life. I. Title.

    BV4910.9.O94 2007
    259'.4196833—dc22

                                                            2007003347

For David, who lived this too

Contents

Acknowledgments

Many people in this book, some named, some anonymous, some pseudonymous, contributed to its contents. Of those, I would like to thank in particular Margaret Harman, Fran and Quanah Adams, Larry and Imojane Snyder, and Glen Darnell for their regular attention to both my parents during this last long passage of my mother's life.

My gratitude is great for the kindness of certain workers at my mother's former nursing home who cared for her and for many others like her, despite inadequate compensation and lack of recognition for the consecrated work they do.

My thanks also go to Lyndie Duff and Fleetwood Range for reading and commenting on early versions of the manuscript, as well as for their constant encouragement.

Finally, I am more grateful than I can say to my husband, David, who submitted with uncommon grace to the demands of caregiving for both my parents and for me.

An Opening Note to the Reader

I had never seen the logic in asking "Why me?" when some calamity befell me. Couldn't one just as reasonably ask "Why not me?" But when my mother developed Parkinson's disease and began to show signs of dementia, I found myself asking on her behalf, "Why her?" If ever a person did not deserve such a fate, it was my mother. She was a good, generous, funny, loving person who had already suffered a number of tribulations in her life. But deserving has little to do with disease. Like the rain, it falls on the just and the unjust. And, as suddenly as a summer thunderstorm, my mother's care fell to me.

In this country, millions of people, most of them women, are living through similar experiences right now. And, except for the occasional PBS special on aging or Alzheimer's, little notice is taken of such a pervasive and well-nigh inevitable human experience. Paul Hogue, director of Harvard's Generations Policy Program, at the 2005 White House Conference on Aging and Policy Committee, provided Congress with the following statistics:

> The first of the baby boomers are celebrating their sixtieth birthdays this year (2006).
>
> By 2030, the number of elderly people in this country will double.
>
> At present, the eighty-five and older population is the fastest-growing segment of the older population.
>
> In 2000 there was twenty-six times the number of people eight-five and older than there was in 1900.
>
> Women will predominate among the elderly, especially among the oldest old. Most of these women will be widows.

These numbers remain abstractions, however, until, usually quite suddenly and with little time to reflect, one becomes the caregiver for an ill and aging parent. My own decision to return to my family home to help my eighty-year-old father care for my mother was more of a reflex than a decision. This is the way most adult children, no longer young themselves, fall into the role of caregiver. Yet no other alteration in life circumstances, with the possible exceptions of marriage or incarceration, changes one's life so drastically.

For me, the move meant geographic dislocation and career disruption. Worse, I had to witness the slow and painful disintegration of the woman who had been, all my life, my model and mentor. No other event during my sixty years shook my faith so deeply.

This book covers the year and a half my father and I cared for my mother at home until her dementia became so severe that keeping her at home was no longer safe for either of my parents. This section includes the difficulty of dealing with a dozen different doctors and the narrowing search for any remedy that might lessen my mother's suffering.

The following five years she spent in that place children and spouses often swear they will never resort to—a nursing home. Since I spent several hours almost every day there, I had ample opportunity to observe and record the special conditions that create the "nursing home culture."

During those years I kept a rough journal, mostly to track doctors' appointments and medications for both my parents. I noted responses to drugs, behavior patterns, and, gradually, I began putting down my own reactions in order to keep from going crazy myself. Eventually I began to structure those notes into a narrative, hoping to find some sense that could be made from what often seemed a chaotic welter.

This is not a self-help book for caregivers. What I hope this book provides is a clear and realistic account of caring for an elderly loved one when the caregiver is nearing the elderly category herself. Also, in consequence, it raises awareness of the spiritual challenges encountered on this path, not least of which are the fears about one's own future disintegration. I consider my experience to be fairly typical, neither the worst-case scenario nor the sunniest outcome. I make a few practical suggestions, but my main intention is to throw light on a rather dark and unexamined corner of our society.

People who are just starting down this path of caregiving might be overwhelmed by reading the book. Others who have put in a few months or years, however, may find comfort in seeing their own experience reflected here. They may also find the questions they have feared to ask or acknowledge formulated for them. C. S. Lewis is reported to have said that we read in order to know we're not alone. In addition, the book may help those foreseeing their own stint at caregiving looming ahead. If this book helps them to anticipate and thus forestall a few of the emotional ambushes along the way, so much the better.

I give as clear an account as I can muster of what dementia looks like and how it affects those who live alongside it. This is not a cheerful book, but it is truthful. It brings to the surface of our busy, active lives a question we usually keep submerged— until some circumstance drags it up and into the light. The question scares us, but dementia forces us to ponder the matter: what makes a being human?

Is it memory, the capacity to reason, volition? When all these are taken away, what are you left with?

Of course, the more immediate and pressing question for a dementia-companion is, How can I live with this person? How can I survive the madness?

During the almost seven years I spent with my mother's dementia, it often seemed as if she were trapped under the rubble of an earthquake, her rationality, curiosity, humor, and generous spirit slowly suffocating under the wreckage of her ruined brain.

All I could do was squat beside the avalanche, listening for any sign of life; sometimes I could hear a faint but familiar echo of her voice or gesture from under the heap. I would grow frantic trying to reach her; how could I let her know she was still loved, still valued? Most of all, I was desperate to reassure her that she was not abandoned there under the rubble.

My mother's dementia was, in the beginning, stroke-related. Later, Alzheimer's was added to her diagnosis, though after a while finding the precise category to put her in had ceased to matter. After a certain point, all dementia begins to look alike.

Nothing had ever confronted so forcefully my faith that an ultimate graciousness dwelt at the heart of the world and cared for us. Watching my mother's mind erode bit by bit challenged my notion of what a human being is.

I have not solved that problem or answered the questions in this book. No mere words can do that. Some questions are so big they can only be lived with, lived in, lived through. What I offer here is a sense of how those questions come and, I hope, a means of clarifying them, a way of putting them into words. Though the words are inevitably inadequate, they are at least markers on the path through this barren landscape. You will know someone has been here before you.

My highest hope, however, is that, while these words will not lessen the anxiety or alleviate the anguish, they will brace you for your own hard vigil. Do what you can to comfort with your presence when there is nothing else to be done. Like earthquake survivors waiting near those trapped in the debris, simply stay.

1

At the Back of the Book

It all started with a phone call.

I usually phoned my mother in Texas a couple of times a week. She was nearing eighty and had been diagnosed with Parkinson's disease the previous year.

"How are you doing?" I would always begin.

"Fine," was her equally routine response. She had always been in good health, always taken care to eat well, exercised regularly, stayed active and engaged. My mother had never been one to complain. She bears up. She manages. She rarely took sick leave during her long working career.

But today she says, "Not so good," in answer to my standard opener.

My grip on the phone instantly tightens. "Oh? What's wrong?"

"I fell."

"Fell?" I repeat. Six months earlier, she had tumbled onto the carpet while bending to make her bed. When her right shoulder hit the carpet, her clavicle snapped in two. The bone had taken all summer to heal and caused her a good bit of pain. For Parkinson's patients, falls are a constant threat, and my mother's osteoporosis compounded the danger.

My own voice is edgy as my questions tumble over one another. "Did you hurt yourself? What happened? Did you go to the doctor?"

"Yes, I went to the doctor," she says testily, as if I hadn't credited her with good sense. "I didn't break anything. They took those—what do you call them? Pictures . . . x-rays. But it's very painful. He said I had bad bruises inside."

I stop myself from pointing out that you can't see bruises on an x-ray. "When was this?"

"Oh, I don't know." Impatient now. "Wednesday maybe. I didn't go for a couple of days. I can still hardly breathe." She sounds suddenly on the brink of tears.

"Why didn't you let me know?"

"Well, there wasn't anything you could do about it, was there? And they didn't keep me in the hospital."

My mind is racing, recording and assessing every nuance, every modulation of tone. Wednesday? Today's only Thursday. "When did you say you went to the doctor?"

"It was after that . . . sometime . . . not right away. I thought I'd be all right at first."

She sounds uncertain about the time, and I consider asking to speak to my father. But he is so drastically deaf he couldn't hear me. I take a deep breath. "Well, I think I probably need to come home, Mother."

"No, no. You don't need to do that. I'm okay now." Still, I can hear uncertainty seeping into her protest.

"I just want to see for myself. Check up on you." I say this lightly, trying to sound as if I'm joking with her. We often play this game—me acting the officious schoolmarm.

But her voice remains stiff, refusing to play her part, as she says, "That'll be fine." Letting me know this is no laughing matter, that when you're seventy-eight with bones that snap like dry twigs, falls are no joke.

The year my mother turned seventy, I took her on a long-promised trip to Europe. She wandered through the British Museum, climbed the stairs in the Anne Frank house in

Amsterdam, scanned the slopes above Salzburg for the dancing figure of Julie Andrews. Through it all, the hunger for such marvels sat naked on her face. I wanted to give this woman the world to which she had first awakened me, the world of art and learning, the one circumstances had denied her.

It was on this trip that the first signs of what turned out to be Parkinson's disease began to manifest themselves, though I failed to recognize them as such. She would hesitate as the subway doors slid open. "Come on, jump!" I'd urge, taking her elbow. I called her slowpoke. Years later, after we discovered how the disease had stifled her muscles' response, I felt rotten about this. But at the time, I was only frustrated that her movements, always swift and sure before, whether at the typewriter or cutting board, were growing awkward and hesitant.

We put it down to age at first. Then last year my husband, whose stepmother had died with Parkinson's, pointed out the way my mother turned.

"Did you notice?" he asked after my parents had come to dinner at our house. "When she turns, she moves her feet in these tiny, jerking steps like the second hand on a clock."

He stood up to demonstrate. "That's just how Ruth moved."

I saw it at once. The Parkinsonian gait is distinctive from a normal elderly shuffle. The previous summer I had taken her for a series of tests at a medical center in Houston to have her growing difficulties diagnosed. All the doctors had studied the computer printouts and declared nothing was wrong, except maybe a touch of arthritis.

Yet even after David's observation, I was reluctant to name my mother's affliction for her. She had a brother-in-law with the disease; already he was bedfast, incontinent, and his speech incomprehensible.

Instead, I scouted out a neurologist who held a weekly clinic in my parents' hometown and encouraged her to consult him, even threatened to make the appointment myself if she didn't. All through the fall and winter she dallied. Then, a few weeks before she knew I'd be coming home for spring break, she called me one morning.

"I've been to that doctor you wanted me to see," she said.
"And?"

"I've got Parkinson's." She paused, and, when she spoke
again, I could hear her voice lift with determination. "I'm all
right though. I'm doing fine. The Lord is going to see me
through this."

I told her how sorry I was to hear the diagnosis and assured
her I would be home again soon. Still, I expected nothing less
than the courage she had always shown.

David and I had already begun discussing in a haphazard
way what the future might hold. I was vexed with myself for not
having already pushed my parents to make alterations to their
home—wheelchair-wide doors, a handicapped bathroom. But
to make those suggestions might sound defeatist now, I worried, as if we were rushing her into invalidism.

These discussions with my husband thus produced little
more than speculation and fretting. The situation seemed too
open-ended for strategizing. My mother's condition could hold
steady for years yet. My father could have a heart attack tomorrow. Each scenario called for a different solution. How, after all,
was it possible to plan?

I had satisfied myself, instead, by accumulating information
about Parkinson's. Fact-finding is my customary mode of coping, the way I convince myself that control, if not easy, is nevertheless possible. I reread *The Man Who Mistook His Wife for
a Hat* by my favorite literary neurologist, Oliver Sacks. I
ordered *The Parkinson's Handbook* from the National Parkinson
Foundation. But as the editors themselves admitted on the last
of its twenty-four pages, the booklet was merely an attempt to
summarize. "Not all the facts about the disease are presented,
nor are the problems discussed fully." Something, I was to discover, of an understatement.

My younger daughter hunted down several back issues of a
Parkinson newsletter published by a group in Kansas City. It
was heavy with articles like "Exercise, Go for It!" and "The
Caregiver's Bill of Rights." Ordinarily, I spurn the self-help
genre, but now I scavenged for facts from articles like "Top Ten

Ways to Live with Parkinson's," which admonished patients ᴗ "eat well," "get some sleep," and "stay informed."

Immediately after her diagnosis, my mother had also begun collecting books with Parkinson's in the titles. These usually contained chapters on the disease's symptoms, most notably tremor, and line drawings illustrating helpful exercises. The last time I had visited, however, I had noticed that these books had disappeared from my mother's coffee table.

"Weren't they helpful?" I asked her.

"Oh," she waved away the question, "they all start off upbeat, you know. How you should just keep going, lead a normal life. But when you get to those chapters in the back of the book," she gave a little shudder, "it's not such a pretty picture."

"Well," I had said then, "we won't worry about that now. We'll cross that bridge when we come to it."

But on this October day as I listened to my mother's jumbled description of her fall that morning, I was recalling that over half of the elderly women who fracture their hips become permanently disabled. Twenty percent die within a year.

But I don't tell her this. Instead, I tell her I love her and that I'll be home that weekend. I put the phone down and pick up my briefcase. At the office I clear my calendar for the following week and glance ahead nervously to the remaining months.

I was afraid that bridge we were going to have to cross was already looming up ahead.

2

Crossing the Bridge

That phone call echoed ominously in my mind during the rest of the day, like the first dislodged pebble that clatters downhill and starts an avalanche.

As I cooked dinner that evening, I called my mother's cousin back in Texas. Margaret and my mother are the same age and grew up together, as close as sisters. They call one another every day. Tucking the phone between my shoulder and ear, I move about the kitchen.

"How's Mother?" I ask as soon as Margaret picks up.

"Oh, dear. You've heard?" Her voice, always pitched high, ascends another notch. "She's not doing too well, honey."

My mother, Margaret says, fell on Monday. She was in one of the extra bedrooms where she keeps her old painting gear and squirrels away gifts for upcoming birthdays and Christmas. She told Margaret she had stumbled over a box, then grabbed for a floor lamp, pulling it over as she fell against the corner of a cedar chest. My father, watching television in the living room, did not hear her fall or her calling to him afterward.

"She says she lay there for fifteen or twenty minutes before he found her," Margaret continues. "She couldn't get up by herself."

Two days later, early Wednesday morning, Margaret came to check on them. She found my mother in bed, obviously in a good deal of pain. She finally talked my mother into going to the doctor. The x-rays showed no broken bones.

"But she's got great big old bruises," Margaret confirms, "all purple and green. The doctor gave her some kind of pills. For pain, I guess."

This worries me. People with Parkinson's have to be wary of mixing medications.

It troubles Margaret too. "She acted a little strange. Said there was someone hiding in the back bedroom and wanted me to go look for them. I asked her who would be hiding there and she said 'the people across the road.' She says she sees them outside at night, packing stuff in boxes. She thinks they're doing something illegal. Drugs or something. And now she thinks they're inside the house."

I slump against the kitchen counter, a knife still in my hand.

"She was whispering all this to me while your dad was out of the room," Margaret continues, "like she didn't want him to know. She said she'd told him about it, but he didn't believe her. I asked her what she thought these people wanted, and she said 'to take away our house.' So I asked her what they would do with her and Lamar. 'They'll just put us out in the woods, I guess,' she said. She wanted me to go back in that far bedroom and look for them."

I find myself fighting a sudden urge to snicker. "So what did you do?"

"I told her I'd go look, but I didn't think there was anyone there. I went back to the bedroom and even got down on my hands and knees to check under the bed—though even a three-year-old couldn't wiggle underneath it, there's so many boxes stuck under there."

I picture Margaret, down on her elbows and knees, poking under the bed for intruders and want to laugh again. "Why, for heaven's sake?"

"I knew she'd ask me if I'd looked under the bed, and I didn't want to lie."

"That's crazy," I protest. "The whole thing was crazy."

"Yes, I guess so. It didn't do any good anyway. When I told her no one was there, she just looked at me like she didn't believe me."

I take a long breath, trying to think. "You say the doctor gave her pain pills?"

"I guess that's what they are. I don't know how many she's taken, or if she's taken any at all. You know how careful she is about mixing her medications."

"Still, that must be it. Maybe there was some kind of inter-action with her L-dopa."

Margaret agrees, meaning to be reassuring.

"But wait," I say, suddenly aware of a discrepancy. "When did you say this happened—the people in the back bedroom?"

"Wednesday morning."

"Before she went to the doctor? Then it couldn't have been the pain pills, could it?"

"No, I guess not." She sounds relieved that I've figured this out for myself.

"I'm coming home," I say. "Daddy can't handle this kind of thing."

"I believe you're right, honey," Margaret says, her voice stronger now. "I definitely think you need to come home."

Home was 554 miles away and up a red clay road to the house at the top of the hill, a house built by my grandfather and deeded to me by my parents two decades ago. Now it's the place our children mean when they say they're coming home—for Thanksgiving, Christmas, funerals. My parents' house is nearby.

My dog Tilly leaps out as soon as I reach my house and open the car door. She wades belly-deep through drifted leaves. Inside my house, the air trembles ever so slightly, like water brimming to the lip of a glass. The windows, all facing south on the ground floor, are light-filled eyes looking back at me, watch-ing to see what I will do. Then, because I know they are expect-ing me before dark, I get back in the car and drive down the road to my folks' house.

Always, when I come home, my mother's face lights up when she first sees me, as though I were a herald of the Second Coming. Always. There would be food on the table, waiting for my arrival, no matter how late. She would have cooked and cleaned all day in preparation, and by now she would be looking out the window every few minutes to see our headlights coming up the lane.

But tonight when I come through the door, for the first time she looks up expressionless from her rocker, then reaches to shift a book slightly on the lamp table beside her, not saying a word. My father rises from his chair, making his customary welcoming noises, but standing back, as usual, for me to greet my mother first.

"Hello, you," I say, and bend down to kiss her. Tilly dashes about the room, then tries to jump in her lap.

"Oh!" My mother cries out.

I speak sharply to the dog, tell her to get down, get away, go lie down.

"Look. Look what she did," my mother says, pointing to an old bruise between the metacarpals, ridged like fan ribs on the back of her hand.

"That spot looks like it's probably been there a while, Mother," I say, making light of it.

"Well, it hurts," she protests in a voice I have seldom heard from her. Then, as if realizing her welcome has not been warm, she adds, "Did you have a good trip?"

I am just beginning to answer when she tells my father she needs to lie down. Avoiding my eyes, he helps her out of her chair and down the hall to their bedroom. I trail behind. She sits on the side of the bed and, as he lifts her feet onto the bed for her, she cries out, "You're hurting me." He still does not look at me.

When he leaves to find her hot water bottle, she pulls up her shirt to show me the bruise on her left side from the fall. Again she tries to describe how the accident happened, her visit to the doctor, the x-rays at the hospital. But the time sequence grows confused and she breaks off.

My father returns and snuggles the hot water bottle against her ribs. Then we leave her to sleep.

In the kitchen, my father, his eyes bent on the dishwater now, tells me in the loud whisper of the hard of hearing, how she sent him up to the attic the previous night, looking for an intruder.

"I explained to her that the doors were all locked," he says. " 'How could anyone get in the attic without our knowing about it, honey?' I asked her." He shakes his head. "She said the man came in through the vents in the roof."

I stare at his lips. They are trembling in jerky little twitches.

He sets the plate he has been washing in the drainer. "I don't know how to handle this kind of thing," he says, bracing his arms against the counter. "I probably shouldn't be telling you all this. I feel like I'm ratting on her."

"No, Daddy," I say, putting my hand on his arm. "I need to know."

"It's not *fair*," he cries out, his voice thick with tears, "it's just not fair for her to get like this."

Fair? I don't know what to say. What does he think this is—a bad call from the Cosmic Referee? Nevertheless, I put my arms around him, oddly gratified by his anger on her behalf.

Back at my house I open a can of soup for me and dog food for Tilly. Then I go upstairs and crawl under the electric blanket, turning the control up as high as it will go. I'm shivering.

"I didn't know it was this bad," I say aloud, startling myself with the sound of my own voice in the darkness.

But it would get worse. It was a good thing I didn't know then just how much worse.

3

What's Natural?

Now it is Sunday morning after my long drive down from Kansas. I force myself out of bed and dawdle over breakfast. Then I whistle for Tilly and head down the road to my folks' house.

My father, washing dishes in the kitchen again, doesn't hear me as I come in. I tiptoe down the hallway to their bedroom. My mother is asleep, making small plucking motions in the air with her hands. She starts to speak, her eyes still closed, but I can't make out what she's saying. After a moment her breathing grows shallow, and she seems to fall into a deeper level of sleep. Her hands grow still. Her mouth is open, her head turned to one side. Her breathing is noisy.

I go back to the kitchen and dry the dishes my father sets on the drain board. As he recounts the times she got him up last night, I murmur sympathetically.

"She insisted there was a fire out in the yard," he says, shaking his head.

I put the last glass away and turn to find my mother standing in the kitchen doorway.

She is frowning and at first I think she must have heard my

father's remarks about her. Then she says, "Did you come over a while ago?"

"No. I just got here, Mother."

"Well, I heard a noise and when I went to look out, there were two little girls playing on the front lawn."

I cast a quick glance at my father. He keeps his eyes steadfastly on the dishwater.

My mother's face lightens as she goes on. "I thought, Oh my goodness, she's brought Audrey and Esther." My two youngest granddaughters.

"No," I say again, more lightly this time, taking my cue from my father who appears bent on ignoring this. "You're stuck with just me, I'm afraid."

The next morning, Monday, I call her family doctor, the same one she and my father have been seeing for the past twenty years. I'm feeling an acute need for more information, fresher facts, and straight from the horse's mouth. But I'm not sure about the protocol in such a situation. Will the doctor even talk to me about my mother's case? In a small town, however, the rules are generally looser, and when I tell him I'm only here for a week, he shows no reluctance to talk.

"She appears to be hallucinating at times," I tell him, and launch into some of the details.

"Mm-hmm, mm-hmm," he interjects, nudging me toward my point.

"So I was wondering if the hallucinations are perhaps a side effect of the medication," I finish, my voice breathy with— what? Guilt? Shame?

With a long, considering sigh, he says, "No. No, it's nothing I gave her. I saw her at the hospital, you know, and all I gave her then was painkillers. And only four or five of those. They're probably all gone by now."

I start to ask him about the medication for Parkinson's prescribed by her neurologist, then stop, realizing he will only refer that question back to the other doctor.

"She did seem a little depressed though," he goes on, "so I gave her a sample package of Paxil, an antidepressant. All the

Paxil does is increase the serotonin. She only has to take it once a day, but it takes about two weeks before she'll see any results."

"I see," I say, not seeing at all. Neither of my parents has mentioned the Paxil.

"I've noticed changes in her the last couple of times I've seen her," the doctor continues, as if wanting to establish his thoroughness. "She seems to be losing weight." He pauses again, then heads back toward the point of my inquiry. "The hallucinations—they're just a result of her deterioration from the Parkinson's. Keep an eye on her. If she gets worse, we may have a psychiatrist take a look at her."

I hang up the phone. A psychiatrist? My mother? Right.

She has, in the past few years, admitted to feeling depressed. "Admitted" being the operative term, as if melancholia were a crime. Consulting a psychiatrist would, in her mind, be tantamount to turning herself in to the authorities. Admitting guilt. Even though she has read that L-dopa, the active ingredient in her Parkinson's medication, can cause hallucinations, to her way of thinking that is no excuse for having them. Just as a low level of serotonin is no excuse for being depressed.

Later, I ask her about the Paxil samples the doctor gave her.

"Those things?" she says with a sniff, not even deigning to name them. "I threw them in the garbage."

Though she worked for years as a medical secretary, my mother has always been wary of medications. Whenever possible, she prefers to let nature take its course. What is and is not natural remains a metaphysical issue for her. In her own lexicon, natural refers to the created order, which by and large expresses God's purposes for the world. Health comes from working within that order. We violate it at our peril.

This philosophy has served her well enough for over seventy years. Until recently, her only illnesses have been colds and flu.

My mother had steadfastly refused hormone replacement therapy for her osteoporosis. To her, substituting an alien version of estrogen after menopause goes against the natural order. Your body, she would argue, stops producing estrogen for a reason—

so you won't go on having babies beyond your ability to care for them. Keeping her hormones at the level of a twenty-year-old woman's is not in line with nature's intentions. Clearly the body will be thrown out of kilter. No good can come of it.

But now her Parkinson's is not only afflicting her body but contesting her metaphysics.

Buried in the brain's core lies a bit of dark tissue called the substantia nigra whose job it is to produce dopamine, a neuro-transmitter that allows messages from the brain to be sent along the nerves to the muscles.

From the time we reach biological maturity, the cells in the substantia nigra are already dying off at the rate of roughly 4 percent annually. That is, if one is healthy and only disintegrat-ing at the normal rate. But for a person with Parkinson's, the cells die off at a much faster clip. Parkinson's patients have typ-ically lost 70 percent of the substantia nigra by the time they are diagnosed.

Though this condition is called a disease, it does not corre-spond to my mother's disease paradigm. She pictures illness as the invasion of a foreign intruder—germs, bacteria, viruses. This concept of an alien agent is important if one is to "fight" disease. But what if there is no invader to target, no enemy to kill off? Even cancer patients have rogue cells, which can be poi-soned or shot with radiation.

In my mother's case, the warfare metaphor doesn't work. There were no foreign bodies or rogue cells to fight. It's her own body that's letting her down. Nor can she ever expect "victory," there being as yet neither cure nor cause known for this disease. The deepest, most essential part of her physical self—her brain—was deserting her, cell by cell, making it even more dif-ficult for her to understand, much less accept, what was happening to her.

My mother's inability to trace her deteriorating condition to a definite origin has left her with a vague sense of guilt. She keeps wondering what food, what chemical in the drinking water, what mysterious airborne agent has caused this condition. What act has she committed or what duty omitted? Where did she go wrong? What could she have done differently?

She insists there must be a reason for what's happening to her. If she's committed no sin against her own body's health, perhaps she's erred in some other way. In her darker moments, she suspects she's being punished for some moral or spiritual lapse.

That mere random chance should pick her out for this indignity is a notion she struggles against. She would rather be guilty than live in a lottery universe. Liability, after all, is the price you pay for believing that order rules the universe. *Natural* means there has to be a reason; cause and effect demands a cosmic quid pro quo.

Bent spines and splintered hips are just as natural to postmenopausal women, I suppose, as pregnancy is to the postpubescent. At my mother's age, death, not life, is nature's aim. Nature thins your bones in order to get rid of you; it's nature's way of showing you the door. Keep asking "what's natural?" long enough, and the answer, eventually, is "death."

Like hormone pills, antidepressants were not "natural." Mental states are a matter of self-control, of will power. To my mother, acknowledging hallucinations meant that she had abdicated responsibility, lost control of the self, that her very soul had somehow failed.

Neither that day, nor for many days to come, would my mother mention to me the people invading her house. In the middle of the night, she would send my father up the pull-down ladder in the hallway to look for men in the attic with their buckets of tar. She would even tell Margaret about the attic invaders. But for some reason, she tried to keep them a secret from me.

Was she afraid of my reaction? Was she trying to spare me? Protect herself? Was there still some place within herself that knew her fears were unfounded, or at least misdirected, and was ashamed?

Delusional was the word I began using to outsiders for my mother's mental state. The term seemed to encompass more than mere hallucinations, those chemically induced modes of perception I remembered from the seventies. Delusional implied a narrative structure underlying such visual aberrations, a story shaped by her anxiety and fears. Hallucinations are random, like clouds forming in the sky. Delusions come from within. Hallucinations might be merely chemical. Delusions are metaphysical.

Neither word, of course, did I use in the presence of my mother.

As I said, I cope by accumulating information, scouring the world for facts. My mother's way was to set her internal logical system in motion, to drill down to the rock core of her philosophical premises.

I was empirical, inductive; she was deductive, operating by precepts. I tend toward Aristotle. She stuck with Plato. The distance between these two ways of coping would cause a chasm to open between us in the months to come. For no matter how many facts I gathered—about medications, brain physiology, chemical interactions—she clung to her belief in the ineffable, unassailable self, an enduring personal identity. Preserving that, after all, was the point of the whole ball game.

Nevertheless, after my first week at home, a strange shift occurred in my own consciousness. I suddenly stopped scavenging for data. I stuck all the newsletters and books about Parkinson's back in a filing cabinet and ignored them. In fact, when I tried to read, I couldn't make sense of the words before my eyes. My brain began to shy away from facts about my mother's disease as if they were red-hot pokers. I would walk back from my folks' house across the fields with Tilly, climb the stairs to my bedroom, and lie down on the floor. Sometimes I would stare out the windows at the tree branches becoming barer every day. Then I'd close my eyes and sleep.

But I didn't read. Nor did I surf the Internet for Parkinson's Web sites. I didn't even think much. In fact, I seemed to have lost the power to think straight. Following a linear train of thought became an impossible task, probably because I was thinking several things simultaneously—or trying to. The past, the future. Kansas, Texas. Parents, children, husband, grandchildren. Work, money, time. No straight lines connected these points. Instead, across the dark sky of my brain burst a shower of fireworks.

I had to constantly remind myself of the most mundane chores, pin mental memos to visual images. "Don't forget this is where you put the car keys," I'd mutter to myself as I dropped them in a tray on the piano bench. Or "Remember when you open the front door to leave, ask yourself if you've turned off the stove." Despite these tactics, I spent what seemed hours searching for keys. Once I came back to a house filled with smoke from a pot I'd left cooking.

The pot wasn't the only thing that burned. I could feel my ganglia smoldering, the soot choking off synapses. My nerve circuits were scorched; in my mind's eye I could see black residue clogging the contact points.

I lay on my bedroom floor, waiting for the blood to pump through my body and carry off the charred bits so I could function again. More than once I thought I might be developing Parkinson's myself, despite my acquired knowledge that the disease is not contagious nor, except for a few instances, was it directly inherited.

Plato was taking his revenge on Aristotle. The old Athenian was showing me just how ephemeral facts are, how little they matter when the citadel of the self is threatened. For the self is the central certainty, the magnet to which all facts adhere. It is the underlying premise on which all our separate realities are built. Without a self, there's no means of either perceiving or interpreting facts. Descartes got it backward; he should have said, "I am, therefore I think." My mother could sense that core within beginning to fracture, and she was terrified.

And so was I.

My mother was a premise in the syllogism of myself. Hers is, after all, the body I came from. Though I knew, empirically, that she had been born in Lovelady, Texas, on March 30, 1920, at an even deeper level I knew her as the archetype that had existed before the foundation of my world.

I had never known a time without her. I might comprehend,

intellectually, that such a time would come when she would disappear from my world. And I could accept—or learn to accept—her absence. But her disintegration, the slow dismantling of her self? And if she, this premise of my existence, splintered, shattered, what did that mean for me? If some obscure centrifugal force could send her sanity spinning off into the vacuum of space, how could I hope to stay whole? If the self goes, what good would a world of facts do me?

The day before I was to return to Kansas, my mother finally revealed her delusions to me. "Listen," she said when I made what had become my regular morning call, "when you come over here, be careful. They poured black tar all over out there."

I was at a loss for how to respond.

"I just don't want Tilly to get tar in her fur." Her voice tightened. "It's getting worse and worse over here every night."

"Okay," I said. "I'll be careful." I punch the off-button on the phone and sit holding it in my hand. Then I dial my office and leave a message that I won't be coming back to Kansas tomorrow.

It's night before I reach David back in Kansas. "I just don't feel like I should leave her right now. She already has Pop jumping through hoops. He doesn't really understand the shape she's in."

"Don't worry," David says. "As close as you two are, just your presence itself helps her."

"Thanks," I say.

"We need to think of this not just as a sacrifice or a duty," he says. "This is the work you're doing now. It's your calling for the present. Your vocation."

I go over to my folks' house to tell them I'm not leaving the next day after all. My mother is in bed. Clumps of hair stick out wildly. Her eyes are sunken and bruised looking.

I sit down beside her and, for the first time, she tells me about the men in the attic with buckets of tar.

"How in the world could these guys get up there?" I blurt out.

"They come in through the louvers at the ends of the roof."

I close my eyes and shake my head.

Her eyes narrow. "Your father said he couldn't find anyone up there, but when he came down, he had black stuff on his feet."

I sit absolutely still. The wall she put up—whether to protect me or to hide from me—has been breached.

Finally she says, "I know you think I'm lying."

Lying? Why does she say lying instead of crazy? "No, Mother, I don't think you're lying. I know this is very real to you." I take her hand. "I think you're feeling a lot of fear and insecurity right now. And it's just taking this form." Then, to reassure her, I say, "I've changed my plans. I'm not leaving tomorrow."

I can see instant relief on her face. Nevertheless she makes a feeble protest. "But you've got your work."

"This is more important. Besides," I try to smile brightly, "I love being here, in my house up on the hill."

She sighs. "I wish I was there too."

I lie down beside her and watch her as she dozes fitfully. Maybe, I think, it will help if we talk about her fears.

When she wakes, I ask, "Are you worried about losing your home, Mother?"

"Not especially," she replies calmly. She likes me there beside her. She sounds like her old self.

Once again, I take a deep breath and feel my chest relax a bit. She sounds so normal, so rational, no fear in her voice. Maybe I've blown this dementia thing out of proportion. Maybe these episodes of confusion are merely transient.

"Good," I say. "That's good. I'm glad to hear it."

She sighs. "It's just that we've never had this experience before," she adds matter-of-factly, "people getting into our house like this."

My brother comes the next month from his home in Santa Fe to take my place so I can spend Thanksgiving with David and our daughters. My brother bakes a turkey and a frozen pumpkin pie for their holiday meal.

When I get back, they are all three—my parents and my

brother—sitting in my living room watching a football game. My brother looks like he's been to the wars. He stares fixedly at the screen, the muscles in his jaw clenched.

Visits from my brother have always gladdened my mother. But not this time. I notice that my mother scarcely looks at him. She seems thinner and the skin around her eyes is dark. Her hair needs washing. She constantly runs her hands through it so that it's flattened on the left side.

When I go into the kitchen to make tea, my brother follows.

"She wouldn't take her Ativan while you were gone," he tells me in a breathless undertone. "Said she wasn't going to take any 'dope.' I found her sitting on the side of the bed in tears. No one believes her, she says. Then she tells me that the people across the road have a smuggling operation." He pauses to rub his forehead.

I nod while I run water into the kettle. This must be what I sound like when I relate the latest incident to Margaret, urgent and affronted by my mother's irrationality.

"Oh. And there's poison gas being pumped into their bedroom. She pointed to her pillow this morning and said, 'Just smell that. You'll see.'"

I shake my head, waiting for the water to boil.

"Then another time I found her up on all fours in the middle of the bed. 'Look,' she says, 'see that snake over there?' I picked up the phone cord and said, 'You mean this?' But she just looked away, like she was shrugging it off." He takes the mug I hand him. "She has *got* to take her medication tonight. We've all got to get some sleep."

That night, with Tilly snuggled against the curve of my back, I think of those chapters at the back of my mother's Parkinson's books that she told me about months ago. The ones with the bad news that caused her to stop reading about her disease.

Is that where we are now? Already at the back of the book?

4

Medicine Men

Despite the fact that Parkinson's disease is no longer rare, my mother's condition had not been accurately diagnosed, even after we had spent months making trips to a diagnostic clinic in one of the best medical centers in the nation. At the end of weeks of tests, the doctors there were still stumped.

But a young neurologist, just revving up his first practice in subleased office space, nailed the diagnosis after only five minutes spent watching my mother walk, turn, and touch her nose with her index finger.

For several years I had been observing medical culture while I sat in waiting rooms, filled out medical histories for my parents, stood beside them in examining rooms, emergency room cubicles, and intensive care units. I had signed consent forms on their behalf, and watched monitors record their test data, so I can see why doctors find diagnosing difficult. Except for the shrinking number of general practitioners, each specialist gets only a piece of the patient to work with.

The patient's body is divided between specialties as touchy about their boundaries as Balkan nationalists. My mother's neurologists got her brain. The orthopedist got her bones and the dermatologist her skin. My father's cardiologist worked on his heart, his urologist his prostate gland.

As time went on, I was making appointments with, accompanying my parents to, and reviewing billings from, a total of twelve different doctors. So focused were all of these doctors on their particular province, that they never inquired about problems in other jurisdictions. Unless I insisted, few ever bothered to check whether the medications they prescribed might conflict with those ordered by other doctors. No wonder diagnoses are difficult; physicians are bred to be isolationists but are working in a global economy.

I got to be something of an expert on physician culture as I observed the medicine men who treated my parents' various ailments. Not only was there Dr. S, their general practitioner (now labeled a PCP for primary care physician), but Drs. P and M, my mother's first and second neurologists, Dr. L, my father's cardiologist, Dr. R, my mother's rheumatologist, Dr. K, my father's urologist, and Dr. H, a dermatologist, as well as various surgeons who only made cameo appearances and a psychiatrist who appeared and vanished from the scene as quickly as a summer storm.

Dr. P wore tassel loafers, laundry-starched shirts, and a cell phone in his pocket. He practiced medicine the way a day trader deals in futures. Fast and pumped.

We saw Dr. P every two months. My mother approached these appointments as if they were tests she dreaded failing. When I arrived to drive her to the doctor's office, I would usually find my father in the laundry room, looking for refuge.

"She's already thrown up her first pill of the day, along with her breakfast," he told me one morning. In the bedroom I find my mother, naked from the waist down, having spoilt her clothes when she lost her breakfast.

"I need something to wear," she snaps. "I can't go like this."

"We'll find something," I say, pushing hangers aside in her closet to find a skirt that will go with the blouse she's wearing.

"I think I have high blood pressure," my mother tells me once we're in the car and on our way to town.

"Well," I say, noncommittally, "we'll see what the doctor thinks."

Dr. P strolls into the examining room, his Bass loafers clicking on the tile floor. "How are you today," he says, scribbling on his clipboard and neglecting his usual handshake.

"That's what you're supposed to tell me," my mother says, half joking, half miffed by his lack of manners.

I smile. He doesn't.

I try to take up the slack by telling him she's been feeling weaker and has gone back to taking a larger dose of Sinemet, hoping this will help. When he looks blank, I add, "Remember? You cut the dosage in half last time."

He frowns. "I did?" He flips several pages back and forth on his clipboard. "Are you sure?"

"Yes," my mother puts in. She is sitting in the tiny room's only chair. She leans forward now, her hands clasped so tightly in her lap her knuckles are white.

"Can you tell any difference?" he asks.

"No, I don't think so," my mother says.

I look at her, my mouth open. "But you said you didn't have the strength to do anything, Mother. That's why you decided to take the larger dosage."

The doctor taps his clipboard with his pen, his eyes darting from me to her.

My mother looks confused now. Everything is going too fast for her to follow. "My pulse—it just races sometimes," she says. "I think it may be the osteoporosis medicine."

The doctor has her climb onto the examining table and roll up her sleeve. He pumps up the armband and listens through the stethoscope, his face trained to immobility. When she asks a question, he jerks the earpiece away, frowning. "Just a minute."

We all watch the red line slowly drop on the meter. "Perfect," he says. "One fifteen over seventy. Textbook."

My mother looks relieved, even happy now. "Well," she says, smoothing her sleeve, "I've never had high blood pressure."

He scribbles out a new script for Sinemet—the large dose—

and shoves it at me, along with the usual invoice to turn in at the appointments desk. "See you in two months."

I look at my watch. Four minutes flat.

Parkinson's patients, because of the slower operating speed of their neurological network, need time—to move, to think, to speak. If they're rushed, the signals between their muscles and their mind tangle in a useless snarl, producing the characteristic tremor. Five minutes may have been long enough to diagnose my mother's symptoms, but it was not long enough to treat them.

When I come over to check on her later in the afternoon, I find her fretting because she can't get her checkbook to balance.

I look at the statement. "Fifty-one cents off? That's not worth the effort of tracking down," I tell her. "Just write it off."

"But," she says, staring at the checkbook, "it's the only worthwhile thing I've done all day long."

Who is to treat this symptom, I wonder, my mother's growing sense of worthlessness?

During that first year, my father had bypass surgery, an adventure rather than an ordeal for him. His cardiologist said he had come through the experience like a man half his age.

After he came home from the hospital, he had to take a mild painkiller for a few days. My mother began to accuse him of being a drug addict.

"He meets up with them down in the woods," she told me one day.

"Meets who, Mother?"

"His drug buddies. One of them has a little dog. A man came to the window on his side of the bed last night—the one with the dog. He tried to get your father to drink a bottle of poison. But I saved him. I took it away from him."

My father described the incident this way: he kept a bottle of water by the bed so he wouldn't have to get up during the night. "She was crying and trying to grab the bottle out of my hand. So I gave it to her. I didn't know what she was talking about."

Those kinds of episodes stiffened my resolve to question Dr.

P, the neurologist, about these fantasies. Although they were the most insidious of my mother's symptoms, I had hesitated to bring them up in her presence. Any allusion to those paranoid phantasms both humiliated her and made her angry.

Driving to my mother's next appointment with Dr. P, I feel obliged to warn my mother that I must finally mention them. I hesitate, trying to find the gentlest name to call them.

"I need to ask the doctor about your . . . confusion."

Her eyes dart toward the side window of the car. "I've come to hate that word," she says in a low voice. She may be crazy but she's not stupid, and she can smell a euphemism a mile away.

In the examining room, I substitute "episode" for "confusion" when I talk to the doctor. And from the inflection of my voice, he immediately understands.

"Oh," he shrugs, unperturbed. "Hallucinations."

My mother sits frozen, staring straight ahead.

"It's the Sinemet," he says. "Goes with the territory. Just a side effect. I'll cut it back. Lowest dosage." He scribbles on his prescription pad. "And here's one for Ativan too." He hands me the two sheets. "For anxiety. Make sure she gets one before she goes to bed. Two if necessary." And he's gone.

The next morning I find my mother in tears. "Your father stole a hundred dollar bill out of my purse to pay that drug dealer," she tells me. "I pleaded with him. I told him how people in the community look up to him. And his grandchildren. How can he let them down? But he wouldn't listen."

My father is outdoors, mowing. I ask him whether she took the Ativan.

"No," he says, taking off his straw hat to wipe his forehead. "She refused. What could I do? Neither one of us got any sleep."

That evening I go over to make sure she takes the Ativan.

"I'll take it later," she says, waving away the little white pill.

"I'm not leaving till you take it," I say, continuing to hold it out to her.

Finally she takes it between the tips of her long, elegant fingers. Then she looks up at me, one eyebrow arched. "Do you need to say any words over it?" she asks wryly.

Going along with the joke, I say, "God bless you, little pill. Help my mother to get a good night's rest." *And the rest of us too*, I think to myself.

That night, for the first time since I came back, I dream about my mother. She is in some enclosed place, but outside, like a walled garden. I am with her. We are sitting together on the grass.

I had had a rather clear picture of myself taking care of my mother when I first came back home. I thought I would drive her wherever she needed or wanted to go, help her with her medications, negotiate through the maze of Medicare and supplemental insurance. She had always been the one who paid the monthly bills, and, if she needed me to take over that job, I would be glad to do that too. I could cook for my parents if need be, or find someone to help with the daily chores. I would talk, read, visit, do whatever would relieve my mother's physical distress and mental anguish. And one area where I was certain I could help was dealing with doctors.

I wanted her to have the best medical care possible, and, since my mother is not an assertive person, I felt I could be her advocate, both researching and speaking up for treatments that would be likely to help her while avoiding unnecessary and fruitless procedures.

But now I was beginning to feel uncertain about my effectiveness in just that area where I had thought I could help the most.

On our next visit to Dr. P, my mother is feeling pretty chipper. She's wearing a fresh white blouse with a new blue wool vest. We only have to wait about twenty minutes, so she's not tired yet and speaks up in a stronger voice than usual when she responds to Dr. P's ritual "How are you today?"

He's still looking at her chart when he says, "So how about the visuals?"

It takes me a moment to figure out that he means the word as code for hallucinations. He glances at me. "Have they decreased with the lower Sinemet dosage?"

Before I can answer, my mother responds. "I haven't noticed any difference," she says.

Has she understood the code? Does she know what he's asking? Dr. P continues his questions in rapid fire, checking my reactions against her answers. What about nausea? Tremor? Weakness? Better or worse?

My mother has difficulty keeping up with the questions, calibrating "better" and "worse" for the different categories he asks about.

Suddenly, he changes directions. "Let's put you on Zoloft for a while, see how that works."

She has no idea what Zoloft is, but her shoulders immediately sag. For her, every new drug is a defeat, even when he explains that, with this, it may be possible to leave off the Ativan eventually.

The cover on the introductory bubble pack of Zoloft proclaims in large letters "For the Treatment of Panic Disorder." He tears it off before handing it to me. His instructions are complicated and require breaking some of the pills in half for the first three weeks.

"Now you won't notice any change for a while," he tells my mother. "It takes a while to build up in the body."

"Like vitamins," I put in quickly.

And here is where my uncertainty comes in. I am colluding with this man to deceive my mother. Whose side am I on anyway?

She leaves the doctor's office looking like she's been whipped, stumbling and shuffling in the classic PD way, pausing to look around every time she changes directions. When we finally make it out to the sidewalk she begins to weep, overcome by what she perceives as failure.

"I'm so useless," she cries, "just so useless."

I put my arms around her. "Don't say that, Mother," I implore her. "We need you, we love you, because of who you are, not what you can do."

"And who am I?" she says bitterly.

I unlock the car—her car—a big Crown Victoria with less

than twenty thousand miles on it, a car she can no longer drive. When I'm behind the wheel I take her hand. It's hot and puffy. I ask if she wants to get some lunch while her prescriptions are being filled. This is how we usually reward ourselves for getting through another doctor ordeal.

But today she just shrugs. "Whatever you want."

That kind of visit to the doctor undermined my confidence. The situation was proving much more complicated than I had envisioned. I was supposed to be my mother's ally in her illness. Yet here I was, in cahoots with an insensitive medical rookie who allots her scarcely ten minutes of his time and treats her as if she's either invisible or an inert tissue specimen. She may have paranoid hallucinations, but she still recognizes that she's being dismissed as irrelevant.

On the other hand, she can't bring herself to admit she hallucinates. Consequently, she withdraws inside her own phantasms. Even mentioning them to the doctor humiliates and angers her. She must feel even more betrayed by me, her daughter, than by the callous and cursory Dr. P.

So whose side am I on here anyway—hers or the doctor's? Shouldn't we all be on the same side? Yet I feel as if I'm wandering in some strange no-man's-land between them both.

Dr. R, I thought, was going to offer a welcome change. At least at first. An orthopedic specialist, he was to treat my mother's constant back pain. She was not enthusiastic when her family doctor referred her to Dr. R. The morning of her appointment she has to be cajoled into climbing into the back seat of the Crown Victoria with my father. He has been obstinate about coming along, though it's clear this does not please my mother. An oversized brown envelope containing her x-rays lies on the seat between them.

The orthopedic clinic is in another town, and the directions have not been particularly clear. When I take a wrong turn, my mother begins to panic. "We'll be late," she wails. My father flinches and mutters to himself.

With no warning, I am suddenly overwhelmed with anger. I want to yell at them both, the way you yell at your kids that you've had enough. In the next instant, I'm angry with myself for not having seen this coming, for not preparing myself to deal with their anxieties.

Dr. R turns out to be even younger than Dr. P, though not nearly so dapper. He sports a disheartening tie and a bad haircut. But he also has a resolutely kind manner. His voice rises and falls in soft, slow cadences, and he nods deferentially to my mother when he speaks to her.

Dr. R looks at the x-rays we've brought, takes some of his own, says he'll need an MRI.

We're back again two weeks later, new photos of my mother's innards in hand, not just her bones, but muscles, the soft tissue of organs, even some blood vessels. Dr. R studies them carefully.

"There's definitely some bulging in these lower disks," he says, "and some bone buildup in the region. Stenosis of the spine. See? The channel for the nerves is narrowed here." He taps on the thick plastic film with his pen.

My father turns up his hearing aid and it begins to squeal.

Dr. R continues, enunciating each word slowly and carefully, "I'd say we have four choices here. First, stronger pain medication. Second, physical therapy. Third, steroid injections to shrink the swelling. And fourth, surgery." He looks at us, smiling benevolently. "Why don't I leave you alone for a few minutes so you can discuss it?"

When he's gone, I hold my breath and sit very still, waiting for my mother to think these options through.

"What do you think we should do, Gin?" she asks, still lying on the examining table.

"Well. You've already tried painkillers and physical therapy," I say and wait.

"I don't want surgery. I don't want that."

My father, standing grimly in the corner, hat in hand, nods with his whole body. He has worn his dentures today, and they're not improving his mood.

"So," I say slowly, "I guess that leaves number three. The

steroid shots." There. I've allowed—or forced?—her to make her own decision.

But when the doctor returns for her decision, we learn that yet another specialist at a pain-management clinic will perform the steroid injection. "It goes directly into the spinal column—a semi-surgical process," Dr. R tells us.

On the drive home my mother sits beside me in the front seat. "I talked to someone recently who had those injections and it didn't do them one bit of good," she says. I can tell by her voice that she is on the point of tears. "I don't expect it will do me any good either."

"Of course not," I say, "if that's your attitude."

"Negative, negative," my father mutters in the back seat. "I never would have made it myself if I hadn't had a positive attitude with my heart surgery."

"They'd better do something for me soon or I won't be around long." My mother sounds angry now.

"People don't generally die of pain," I say. For a moment I savor the satisfaction of my spite. Then just as suddenly I am appalled. How could I have said such a thing? Once more the question rises up to accuse me: whose side am I on anyway?

What reason, after all, does my mother have for optimism? She had started with a fair amount of hopeful trust in her doctors. It is in her nature as well as her cultural conditioning to trust the medical experts. But not any more. None of the prescribed medications or treatments have alleviated, much less cured, her condition. My father's team won. Hers is losing. All I'm doing is sitting in the stands.

And as it turned out, my mother was right. The steroid injections did her no good.

I dream that night of three pine trees growing between my house and the road. A big wind came up and sheared off the tallest one, blowing it into the field across the road.

I tell myself that I ought to be used to this by now. It's been seven months since I came back to help care for my mother. But the anger and frustration are catching up with me. Nothing is as simple as I had dreamed it would be. My mother is broken and the medicine men, it appears, can't fix her.

If I could just stop hoping, stop even wanting, for her to get better.

My father says she often begs him, "Please don't ever leave me." How do you get used to that?

Between them, my parents were now up to a dozen doctors. Which meant not only juggling appointment schedules but monitoring changes in medications and retrieving reports on lab work and x-rays. Each doctor, each facility, sent separate billings, all of which had to be checked against Medicare and supplemental insurance statements. None of these entities—doctors, labs, hospitals, government agencies, or insurance companies—deal directly with one another. They send out bills and statements like sovereign states issuing fiats. The patient or the patient's surrogate must reconcile their differences, like a diplomat shuttling between continents.

As for Medicare, each statement announced in bold letters: STOP MEDICARE FRAUD! This admonition was followed by instructions to check your billing carefully. While Medicare paid up in a timely manner, my mother's supplemental insurance lagged behind in its payments several months. Debt collectors began calling my parents' home about bills that had not been paid. I spent hours on the phone every week, sorting out these problems.

Several more months went by. My mother called me early in the morning now, sometimes during the night, begging me to come get her. They had been locked in the house by enemies, they had no lights, wild Indians were after them. My father, suffering from complications following prostate surgery, was beside himself with worry and lack of sleep.

Then my hometown got another neurologist. I made an appointment, hoping anew that this doctor would be the one who could help my mother.

Dr. M, like Dr. P and Dr. R, was young. I had by then come

to see the benefit of having boy doctors, however, especially in a field such as neurology where fresh training counts. Dr. M spoke with an Indian accent—something between a chant and a chirp. He was appalled that my mother had not yet had an MRI scan of her brain and scheduled one for the following week. She was beginning to show signs of aphasia, often circumlocuting her way around blank spots in her shrinking vocabulary.

With no hesitation, Dr. M asked her if she experienced hallucinations.

"No," she says.

He turns to me and my father. I simply nod once.

My father clears his throat and phrases his answer with care. "I can't say that I always see the things she does."

At the end of the exam, Dr. M gives my mother a hearty pep talk in his clipped, precise consonants.

"You must get out more. Be among people. Observe the changing seasons." As though to invite her attention to the late winter landscape, he waves his arm toward the wall where a window might have been if this weren't an examining room. "We are going to make your life better. But you must find a purpose!" he exhorts.

Strangely enough, Dr. M's motivational message appears to have worked, perhaps better than he intended. Both my parents left his office convinced that my mother is going to be cured.

Fine, I think to myself. Whatever works, even if it's only temporary.

This upbeat attitude lasts till I take my mother to the hospital for her MRI the following week. She lies, cold and stretched as flat as her bent back allows, on a narrow board that slides soundlessly into what looks disconcertingly like a white plastic coffin.

Meanwhile, in the waiting room I study a pamphlet describing the process of magnetic resonance imaging. The human body, it says, is mostly fat and water, both of which are made largely of hydrogen atoms. In fact, about 63 percent of the body is hydrogen atoms. The big white cylinder holding my mother is itself an immensely powerful magnet. When the technician shoots the juice to it, a magnetic field is created, thirty thousand times stronger than the earth's. Responding to that magnetic pull, each of the protons at the heart of my mother's hydrogen atoms will point in the same direction, like billions of little compass needles aiming north.

Next, the machine stimulates her body with radio waves that will change the steady-state direction of these magnetized protons. Then it cuts off the radio waves and records the pattern of waves bouncing back from her polarized protons. From this pattern the radiologist will read the map of my mother's brain.

When my mother slides out of the cylinder, I half expect her to look like a member of the Star Trek crew being beamed aboard the Enterprise, gradually reassembling their molecules. But she hasn't been stirred into a cloud of twinkly lights. In fact, she's so weak that she submits for the first time to transport by wheelchair out to the curb.

"The noise," she cries, "it was like a jackhammer on my head."

The MRI pictures tell Dr. M. what he expected—that my mother has had a number of small strokes. "Lacunar not embolisms," he emphasizes, "in different regions of the brain. On both sides of the brain. Also in the basal ganglia and the brain stem."

I make a mental note to look up these terms on the Internet.

"You see," he says, settling into a didactic mode, "hallucinations are caused by the introduction of strange chemicals into the brain. But other sorts of deficits—confusion, not being able to tell time, for instance, or aphasia—this is caused by stroke and the damage done to neurons."

I nod, glad to discover these are two separate effects with different causes. It seems to me an important distinction, this line between aberration and deficit. But does it tell us something about the self, other than what unstable mechanisms we humans are? Minute amounts of caked white powder, less than the salt you might sprinkle on an egg, can unhinge the self from other people's reality—the world other people perceive.

"What we are going to do, I think," Dr. M continues in his singsong accent, "is make sure she takes an aspirin a day. Also, maintain the lowest Sinemet dosage, but increase to three times a day the drug I prescribed last time."

He rips off the sheet, hands it to me, and turns his encouraging smile on my mother. "See you in three weeks." He bows formally to my father. Then, awkwardly, as if the gesture is not natural to him but one he is determined to learn, he sticks out his hand for a shake.

A friend suggested that an acupuncturist might be able to help my mother's back pain. "The one I go to has sure helped me," she testifies.

In desperation, I make an appointment for my mother at the China Acupuncture Clinic in town. Reluctantly, she agrees to go in order to satisfy her friend.

Priscilla Wong is a slender, middle-aged woman, about my height, who sounds more kindly in person than on the phone. When I called to make the appointment, her words erupted in short, rapid explosions as if she were barking at me. Face to face, however, I can see how the corners of her eyes crinkle when she smiles.

The China Acupuncture Clinic is housed in what used to be the town's post office when I was a child. Its uneven floor is covered now with indoor-outdoor carpet. The accommodations are somewhere between unpretentious and stark.

Dr. Wong's assistant is a tall, thin man who also speaks in abrupt blasts, ending every phrase with an interrogative "okay?" as if goading you toward some questionable agreement, a tone that creates a certain suspicion in an American hearer.

Dr. Wong, her assistant, and I manage to get my mother up and onto her stomach on what looks like a massage table. After positioning a number of small pillows around and under her body, they stick long thin needles into her lower back, buttocks, and down both legs with quick, deft jabs. Finally, they attach two of the needles right above her forehead. These look like little horns. To all these filaments they connect wires from a machine about the size of a short keyboard and turn a knob, adjusting an electric current.

"You feel tingle, okay?" Dr. Wong says. "Not hurt. No pain. If pain, I turn down. Okay?"

My mother doesn't respond, not even to a string of "okays" shot at her by Dr. Wong's assistant as the knob is slowly advanced.

The pair leaves us for twenty minutes, turning down the lights before they go. "Just relax, okay?"

When the twenty minutes are up, the man returns and removes the needles, after which he massages her back vigorously. Then he has her sit up and swing her legs over the side of the massage bed, facing him. He grasps the sides of her head between his hands. He closes his eyes, takes a deep breath and presses his forehead against hers. For a minute or more he holds her like that while he breathes heavily.

"He transfer energy," Dr. Wong whispers to me. She smiles encouragingly at my mother whose eyes are fixed on the man.

"He sending his spirit into her," Dr. Wong whispers.

I nod, hoping my mother hasn't heard this.

At last the man releases her head and grins, as if trying to underscore his beneficent intent.

"What was that man doing?" my mother demands when we climb back in the car. She has said little else during this long procedure. "What was he doing to me anyway?"

Her friend, who has gone with us to the clinic, attempts an explanation of Asian medical practices.

"But what was he doing?" my mother repeats.

"I guess you could say it was like praying. In a way," her friend says. "Maybe that's what happens when we pray. We transfer the energy of our spirits to someone else."

Now my mother is no materialist. Indeed, she believes wholeheartedly in the numinous. Which is why she is so rattled by this energy-transference business. Whether you call it transferring energy or praying, the act was shockingly intimate. Dr. Wong's assistant might just as well have offered to loan her his underwear.

"But I don't want his spirit," my mother says.

My mother and I go back to the China Acupuncture Clinic two more times. Dr. Wong's assistant never tries to transfer his energy again. In the end, we both agree that, since her back pain has not lessened, we will not return.

Acupuncture had been my last grasp at a straw that might have at least provided some relief from pain. Now I felt as if I had entered the long corridor of medical fatalism. I can't make Eastern acupuncture work any better than her Western medications.

Dr. M was not fully satisfied with the results of my mother's MRI. He orders another test, this one at his office and considerably more high-tech than the acupuncture gizmo.

Two dozen electrodes that will measure my mother's brain waves are stuck to her skull with an oozy gel. The technician, impressed that I know the occipital lobe from the temporal, lets me watch the computer screen as it records the activity inside my mother's head. I had feared the wires leading from her scalp to the machine might look sufficiently like the acupuncture device to put her off, but, as soon as she lies down on the table, her eyes close and she seems to fall instantly asleep.

"Blue's for left, red's for right," the technician tells me, pointing to the monitor where a dozen or so graph lines begin to crawl across the screen.

I nod as if I know what the colored lines mean, but I'm really keeping an eye on my mother. The fine grain of her pale skin glistens with a dew of sweat. The flesh that sags into wrinkles when she's upright is smoothed back from her fine bones and thin nose to reveal the face I remember from better days. The loss of her serene and austere beauty, hidden away in the bones the way her singular self is obscured by phantasms, makes my throat suddenly tighten. My eyes burn with tears I blink back.

"Dr. M was born in Kuwait," the technician confides. "But he's Indian. His father's a banker. Did you know?"

At that moment Dr. M himself comes through the door, glances briefly at the red and blue lines creeping across the screen, then tells me to cut my mother's Zoloft in half. "We'll gradually take her off altogether," he sighs. "It could be affecting her paranoia. Too much dopamine, you know, produces schizophrenia."

No, I want to shriek, I didn't know. And why hasn't anyone told me this before now?

But I say nothing. I have worked hard to establish my intelligence with Dr. M so that he will indulge his marked pedagogical streak and supply me with more medical details than I am likely to get elsewhere.

Most doctors, I have found, brush aside requests for precise information. "It's complicated," they say with a sigh and shake their heads. And if you persist in your inquiries, they can get prickly. Too much curiosity, too much knowledge, and the doctor may perceive you as a threat.

With my own doctor, I can afford to be stubborn, badger him for more information. But if the medicine man treating your mother is the only specialist in three counties, you can't risk offending him.

So you grow devious, pretend helplessness. "Is there some way I might . . . ?" "Can you suggest . . . ?"

The dance between doctor and patient—not to mention doctor and patient's child—is a delicate minuet, one you must often perform cloaked in deception.

In this long, slow dance with my mother's medicine men, I have been anxious about usurping her prerogatives. I want her doctors to speak directly to her. I want to stay in the background, supplying information when it is needed, taking note of instructions the doctors give her. I want, in other words, for her to be treated like a person and not the mere object of scientific inquiry. Instead, for the most part they ignore her and direct their questions and comments to me.

I have tried to circumvent that by making sure my mother sits right under the doctor's nose and, when he asks me a question, I take pains to redirect it to her. If one is insistent and sufficiently unsubtle, the doctor usually gets the point and makes an effort to play along, at least at the beginning. But it doesn't take long for him to grow frustrated. Sometimes my mother has a hard time understanding the question and is slow to respond. Sometimes she just looks helplessly at me, unable to frame a reply. Once she just shrugged and said with unmistakable bitterness, nodding at me, "Ask her." And sometimes her replies simply sound irrelevant. Then the doctor frowns and turns back to me. And so I become an accomplice to these doctors in the objectification of my mother.

I understand the doctor's frustration. He is working with a woman who either can't or won't reveal her secrets, a woman who sees him as the enemy.

After my mother and I leave these exams, I recapitulate the visit, hoping it will help her remember his instructions, explain again any new information about her condition. But she isn't fooled. She knows she is the bug under the microscope.

So I also understand my mother's disengagement from her own treatment, even though it frustrates me. I sympathize with her reluctance to cooperate, even as it angers me. After all, nothing has changed, at least not for the better. And, the way she sees it, each visit is a test she flunks by failing to get well.

Trying to do it right, by the book, trying to match the reality of our situation to the ideal of the experts—the effort wearies me. We speak easily these days of miracle drugs, miraculous cures. We demand that physicians perform feats for which no mortal should be held accountable. *Heal us*, we cry. *Save us. Don't let us die!* And we believe, we actually believe, they can.

So, unfortunately, do they.

But my mother is losing her medical faith. She goes to the doctor the way I went to church as a teenager, bitter and under duress. She takes her pills like an apostate receiving communion, with little hope in their efficacy. A dark night for both soul and body.

5

Demented

In Dante's *Inferno*, Virgil warns Dante as they begin their descent into hell, "We have come to the place where I have told thee that thou shalt see the woeful people, who have lost the good of the understanding."

The inscription Dante reads over Hell's gate is likewise disheartening: "Before me were no things created, unless eternal, and I eternal last. Leave every hope, ye who enter!"

Those words from the inscription are probably Dante's most famous. But just what are those eternal elements he says were made before Time? Not the body, certainly. Within its very genes ticks the timing device programmed for its destruction. And what of the mind? Does it hold up any better to time's erosion?

My mother was losing the good of her understanding. She became one of the woeful people. She abandoned hope. She entered the hell of dementia.

Witnessing her dementia for the first time had been like slamming full force into a closed door. During my first year of caring for my mother, her sanity foundered like a ship battered against a craggy shoal. And all I could do was watch its splintering disintegration. The lifelines I tried to throw out to her fell short. My attempts at rescue all failed.

At times I feared I might go under myself. I spent hours flat on my back, splayed out on my bedroom floor. I felt as if the universe had come unhinged. How could this have happened to the person from whom I had learned everything fundamental to life? The one who had taught me to seek truth, love, and beauty, to pursue justice? Caught in this hurricane, I felt my anchor giving way down in the depths of a cold interior sea.

I often fell asleep there on my bedroom floor. Every time I woke, day or night, I had the same sensation one does after some great catastrophe. On the moment of waking, everything seemed normal again. Nothing had happened. It was only a bad dream. Then it would hit me. The bad dream was real. A trapdoor opened under my feet and I plunged into darkness again.

Cousin Margaret had worked for three years as the daytime companion for an elderly woman with Parkinson's.

"Don't worry," Margaret would console me. "These things go in spurts. Esther probably won't get any worse for a while. Wait before you make any decisions."

I hadn't kept a journal for years, but I began then to record medications, doctor's appointments and instructions, research notes, conversations. Uncertain what might prove important in her treatment, I scribbled everything into one notebook till it was full, then opened and dated a new one. I wrote to track the progress of my mother's disease but also because, without crushing this psychic chaos into material words, I would have lost my own mind.

My firsthand observations of my mother's behavior at that point could be summarized thus: She had hallucinations, most often visual. She saw people anticking around fires across the road at night, a man hovering threateningly at her bedroom window, black holes opening before her in the bathroom floor. A little dog slept on her bed. Tar was mysteriously tracked through the house and clung to my father's feet. Mud seeped up through the carpets. The world she saw was full of slime, darkness, and threat.

Her memory, at that point, was unaffected. Unless, of

course, you count the fact that she remembered events that never actually happened.

She was depressed, though I didn't necessarily take this to be a sign of mental instability. Who wouldn't be depressed, in her condition?

My mother had, as we say, good days and bad days. Ups and downs. Like a roller coaster. Some days she seemed almost her old self again. We could joke or gossip, write notes, recount news from phone calls. During the first few months she still paid bills and balanced her own checkbook. On particularly good days, I could coax her out of the house to visit friends or shop.

But the good days only made the bad ones worse. Inevitably, those lucid days lured me into hoping she had caught her mental balance. Watching her pull weeds from the flower bed or listen attentively to an old friend's conversation, I would think, she's not so bad after all.

With visitors especially, she could maintain all her old social graces. No one seeing her and my father together in their usual pew at church would have suspected anything was wrong. Her friends knew she had Parkinson's disease and noticed her slow, deliberate movements. But they had no idea of the wild, sleepless nights, the hallucinations, the irrational fears and uncontrollable terrors lived out in that house.

As time went on, the good days grew rarer and the roller coaster's dives more precipitous. Any hope that sprouted one day was uprooted the next.

"If only," I told Margaret, "she could just get bad and *stay* that way. It's this backing and forthing that's driving me crazy."

Once, many years ago, I was in an automobile wreck. I remember the car lurching from side to side, rocking up on the wheels until it finally flipped over. The way we were ricocheting between the twin poles of lucidity and dementia felt like that car wreck to me.

What did it feel like to her? Did she realize what was happening? Was she aware of her own condition?

That's a harder question to answer.

Whenever my father had to be gone overnight, I stayed with her, sleeping in the same back bedroom which for thirty years I'd occupied on visits home. Back then, coming home for visits had always been a treat. My father would put a rose cut from my mother's garden on the nightstand for me. My mother would cook my favorite dishes. They spoiled me then as they never had when I was a child. When the old hobnail bedspread in the guest room grew a little shabby, I wouldn't let them buy a new one. I wanted home always to stay the same. Now, when I slept in that bed, it was not as a guest but as my mother's keeper.

Around midnight I would hear her stirring. I would lie in the dark, holding my breath. Then it would grow quiet again and I would drift back to sleep. Around two in the morning, however, she might come into my bedroom.

"Gin," she would say, "you've got to get up. Someone's trying to get in the house."

"No, Mother. Go back to sleep. It's nothing." I would try to keep the irritation from my voice.

But she would stand in the doorway, backlit by the hall light, her breath coming short and hard. "All right," she'd say, her voice breaking as it rose, "you'll see when we all burn down."

So I would get up, slowly, acting out my annoyance.

She'd shuffle toward the front door and point across the street. "See those lights over there?"

"No, Mother. There's nothing there. I told you. Now go back to bed."

She'd look at me then with furious incredulity.

"All right," I'd say, turning away. "Suit yourself. Stay up if you like, but I'm going to bed."

This is not the correct way to treat someone with dementia. This was the act of a desperate and disappointed child who is forced to become the parent.

At such times, I am certain my mother was convinced of the reality of her visions. She refused to be reasoned out of her hallucinations. In her mind, we were bent on discrediting those visions and thus consigning her to inconsequence.

Back in my own house, I tried to reason with myself. Just

how much sense does it make anyway, expecting a crazy person to listen to sense?

"Crazy" is not a word that doctors use. It won't appear on a patient's chart. The accepted term is "dementia." Or, more specifically, "delusional states." I used that one a good bit at the beginning of my mother's downward spiral. An even more medically precise term for her plight is "delirium," though scarcely anyone uses it, no doubt because of its association with alcohol withdrawal.

But "crazy" is the word I said to myself. A word that can carry a greater load of cosmic anger than the more professional synonyms. A term that's strong enough to break through the fog of denial. I repeated it in order to face the fact that a woman as sensible and self-composed as my mother, the person I relied on for advice and trusted for both truth and love, could turn into a madwoman.

She who had been so fastidious about her person, the icon I had watched dressing for work in her starched white blouses and pearl button earrings, now wandered from the kitchen to the bedroom in slovenly smocks, hair askew, refusing to bathe sometimes for days.

I grope for a word that will contain this present reality while maintaining the authentic past, a word that will not dishonor that truth, sully her memory.

My father, though he directly suffered far more from her wild accusations and nighttime wanderings than I, could never bring himself to name this darkness at all. He would describe or narrate an incident, sometimes even gesture with a forefinger to his head, but never simply name, never designate it with a single word. To name would be to make her dementia unbearably real, and worse, to betray her.

But alone, and to myself, I said "crazy." Cracked. Broken. The analogy is with porcelain, a glossy surface fractured into a web of fissures.

"People are always asking how Mother is," I told David. "I just want to shout at them—'Crazy, that's how. Can't you see? The woman's stark-staring mad.'"

They would not have believed me. Maybe that's why I felt like yelling it at them. Because whenever my mother went out among people, or even on those occasions when people came to see her at home, she would call upon some deep reserve of will power, pull herself together, and murmur the phrases worn smooth from years of use. So good to see you. Oh my goodness. Fine, thank you. I never ceased to marvel at this ability.

I understand it is not uncommon for people with almost any form of dementia, even Alzheimer's patients in their early to middle stages, to conceal successfully the gulf between their reality and ours.

My friend Lee says her father's dementia comes from seventy years of solitary drinking. "Daddy doesn't know where he is half the time," she complained. "But let company come and you'd never guess he has any problem. He's just as polite and charming as ever. When I mentioned to his niece that he thinks he still lives in Houston, she looked at me as if I'd lost *my* mind."

That exasperation, I know from experience, comes from wondering how a parent can fake lucidity for the public but not for you. And where, in what part of that damaged brain, does the demented one not only figure out what is "appropriate" behavior but that now is the moment to display it? Doesn't that maneuver require some sort of rationality?

My mother's facility for social concealment made it difficult to determine whether my mother was aware that, as she would have put it in better days, she "was losing her mind."

She distrusted my father and me a good deal more than she doubted her own inner world. But then, who doesn't put more faith in their private perceptions than those of other people? It would be crazy not to.

One day, making her way to the bedroom for a nap after lunch, my mother stopped and watched me putting dishes in the sink. I could feel her long fingers tremble as she took hold of my arm.

"I'm so glad you're here," she said, and her eyes filled with tears. She struggled to keep them from spilling over. For a long moment she hesitated as if she might add something else.

I waited, hoping she might give some sign that she knew she was fighting for her sanity. But she said nothing more, so I kissed her and told her I loved her. She nodded, turned, and went on her shuffling way to bed.

Later that day, walking home, I wondered what it was she might have said. Had she been on the point of telling me about her fears? Should I have probed?

A woman in our church who had recently suffered a stroke, told me about the Heritage Program at our local hospital. "It kept me from losing my mind," she testified. "Sort of a support group. It might help your mother too."

I was growing susceptible to well-intentioned suggestions, since my own efforts to keep my mother sane weren't working. Just getting out of the house might do her good, I thought. She'd at least get to talk to someone other than her deaf husband and her badgering daughter.

The following week I announced to my mother that a young lady was coming to visit her. "From that program at the hospital I told you about. They have to interview you before you can sign up."

My mother had always been a great promoter of projects to benefit the community. Ten years earlier she had solicited funds from local businesses to pay for lighted markers so the fire department could locate hydrants at night. Another time it was a device to keep deer from being hit on the highway. In earlier, happier times she might have invited someone from the Heritage Program to explain their work to her women's club.

Now she looks at me suspiciously. When I go on too long, too enthusiastically about the program's benefits—of which I myself am skeptical—she settles back in her green rocker and says stonily, "When?"

Fortunately, the young woman is stocky, athletic, and a trifle bouncy, though not so much as will put my mother off. Claudia asks my mother questions about her illness, her past, her feelings about her disabilities. I sit back by the fireplace, adding or modifying information when I'm asked. Then, as if wrapping up the session, Claudia says, "I have to give you this little test, Mrs. Stem. I hope you don't mind. It doesn't determine whether you are accepted into the program. It only helps us place you in the proper level."

Uh-oh, I think. Here comes the hard stuff.

Because I have been researching the topic, I know that the questions Claudia asks are taken from the Mini-Mental State Exam for Alzheimer's screening.

With the first section my mother does pretty well. She knows the day of the week, the month and year, though she's hazy about the specific date. She knows the town, county, and state she lives in, as well as the name of the current president. She can name a watch and a pencil, but has trouble spelling "world" backward and is overwhelmed by the task of counting backward from one hundred by sevens.

Claudia hands her a piece of paper, asks her to take it, to fold it in half, and then to place it on the floor. My mother carries out this three-stage command with no hesitation but some bewilderment. She stumbles a bit repeating the phrase, "No ifs, ands, or buts."

When Claudia congratulates her on doing well, she is caught between feeling relieved and suspecting that the young woman is condescending to her.

But candidates for this hospital nirvana have yet another hurdle to jump before they are accepted. An interview with a psychiatrist. You might as well say rattlesnake to my mother as psychiatrist.

"Psychiatrist," broken into its Greek components, means "soul-doctor." And though she does not know Greek, my mother knows when her soul is being trifled with. She lacks the current reverence for secular experts in such matters. Trying to prepare her for this event, I substitute the word "doctor" for psychiatrist whenever I can, but my mother is not fooled. She knows she's up against a trial of her sanity.

The next week I push my mother's wheelchair out of the elevator onto the third floor of the hospital and down the hall to

Dr. W's office. He is wearing jeans, cowboy boots, and a white lab coat. I sit down beside my mother's wheelchair during the preliminary questions.

Then Dr. W asks me to leave the two of them alone together. I am only too happy to escape across the hall to the staff lounge. After a time I am called back in. The psychiatrist goes over some information with me to confirm details, then nods, gets up and leaves, calling out directions to a nurse as he goes.

In her wheelchair, my mother sits stiff with disapproval. Her nostrils are flared. "He didn't even excuse himself," she tells me. "What kind of manners is that?"

The doctor prescribed daily sessions at the Heritage Program for my mother, but she only agreed to three mornings a week. She refers to these group meetings, entirely without irony, as her school. It's her way of either making sense of the effort or saving face. Probably a little of both.

Every other morning I haul the wheelchair in and out of her car's capacious trunk and push her up to the hospital's third floor. The first day, while the nurse is weighing my mother on a lift contraption, I listen to the discussion going on around the table in the program's meeting room. Half of the dozen or so people at the table are in wheelchairs. Two look to be younger than I; one of them has MS, the other a spinal cord injury.

Claudia, the young woman who came to interview my mother, is holding up the morning paper for the people around the table to see.

"Okay, who thinks President Clinton should be impeached?" she asks.

A few of the people look out the window. Some frown at the question as if they are considering. Others talk to their neighbors. None seems particularly interested in the issue of impeachment.

At noon, when I come to pick my mother up, they are all eating lunch around the same table. My mother looks up from her sandwich, and seeing me, her face relaxes in relief.

After the first two weeks I arrange for the hospital van,

equipped with a wheelchair lift, to pick my mother up. Since several other "students" are picked up and delivered this way, however, the trip is a long one for my mother. She begins to complain of back pain from having to sit too long in her wheelchair.

I resume taking her myself, but the next weekend she says to me on the drive home in a voice at once careful and so nervous it quakes, "I know this is probably going to hurt your feelings, but I don't want to go back to that thing at the hospital any more."

I nod.

"Sitting there so long—it just hurts too much."

I nod again.

"And I need to go to the bathroom. It's not easy there. You have to ask."

"I understand."

"Besides, they just go over the same material every day, and the same people repeat the same old things over and over."

As I understand it, that is the nature of support groups. The truth is I haven't been particularly impressed by the program myself. The promised art and music sessions I had used to lure my mother into trying the program have not materialized. The grant money that provides jobs for at least five staff people and no doubt gives Dr. W a healthy supplement to his income, seems little more than a baby-sitting service for disabled adults.

"I completely understand, Mother. If you don't feel it's doing you any good, you certainly aren't obliged to go."

She sits back and sighs. "I just feel like I don't have much time left and I don't want to spend it in a hospital."

Five months later, my mother would lose the cognitive skills needed to answer the questions in Claudia's Mini-Mental State Exam. She could not spell "world" either backward or forward nor count from one to ten, much less backward by sevens. She couldn't tell you what day it is or if we have a president.

Did I care that she had lost the ability to spell and count? Of course not. Illiteracy is not hell. But constant terror is.

6

Spent Light

Back when I was still living in Kansas, around the same time my mother was diagnosed with Parkinson's, I began noticing spots on my glasses. A dozen times a day I would take them off and try to rub off some stubborn speck. After weeks, maybe months, I finally decided there must be a flaw in the prescription. On my next trip to Texas, I decided, I would have my optometrist check this out. Months went by, however, before I got around to scheduling the exam.

My optometrist is a thin man with a gently cautious manner. He wheeled his stool over to me, flipped down a paper paddle in front of my eyes, and said, "See that grid of black lines like a tic-tac-toe game? Okay. See that little dot in the middle? Focus on the dot and tell me what happens to the lines."

"The lines disappear," I said.

He cleared his throat. "Okay. Let's try something else."

He put me through several more tests, then peered inside my eye with his super-beam light. After a while I heard him mumble "macula."

I went home reeling. The previous summer I had met a woman with macular degeneration. She must have been seventy and her older brother was leading her along a path in the foothills of the Rockies, describing the view to her. I knew that people with macular degeneration eventually go blind. What I didn't know was how long it took. Or that the disease was incurable.

When David got home I showed him a time-lapse video I'd found on the Internet purporting to replicate various stages of the disease. We watched the monitor as the black center in a circular photograph of a sunset gradually spread till it blocked out the entire picture.

How much longer would I be able to read? Or to write? Or drive? The dread of those and other losses began to hit me. How, after all, would I take care of my mother if I couldn't see?

The optometrist scheduled an appointment with a retinal specialist. I checked government agency sites on the Internet for state and federal definitions of legal blindness. Disability insurance provisions. Programs for training seeing-eye dogs.

Unlike my parents' many physicians, Dr. H was an older man. What hair remained to him was streaked with gray, and the shoulders of his dark suit jacket were dusted with a light fall of dandruff.

"No," he said, after peering into my dilated eyes. "It's not macular degeneration."

I drew in a trembling breath of gratitude.

"But you do have another condition." Instead of naming it, he had his nurse give me an injection of dye, then took some two dozen photos of the inside of my eye, using a light so powerful it left me weak with pain and panic. He measured my intraocular pressure—24 p.s.i in the right and 18 in the left.

"What's normal?" I asked.

"Well, anything under twenty is . . . okay." He paused. "But everyone is different, you know."

Over the next nine months, Dr. H tested me with a number of strange devices, put me on an extremely low-salt diet, and prescribed eye drops to lower the intraocular pressure.

None of these did I mention to my mother. She had just started a new medication herself and was becoming weaker. I had been so relieved to hear I didn't have macular degeneration that I didn't worry much about what this as-yet-to-be-named problem might be.

So when a friend asked after church one day, "How are you doing—with your eyes," I stared at her blankly.

"Fine, I guess." I hadn't really had time to think about it.

My anguish about my mother was at its most acute stage then. She now realized, at least most of the time, what was happening to her. She was losing her mind, and, in some part that she still retained, she was aware of that terrifying fact.

She had begun demanding bottled water, convinced that something in their well water had caused her Parkinson's disease. In an effort to combat these fears I had sent a sample to a state agency for analysis.

After the test results came back negative for any known risk, she said to me one day, "I've told your father not to bother about buying bottled water any more. I'll just drink the well water."

"Because the test showed it's safe?"

"No. Because it just means I'll die sooner," she said, and started to laugh, more naturally than I'd heard her do in months.

The next week I took her for her regular dental check up. As we were leaving, she said, with feigned nonchalance that she wouldn't be going back there.

"What do you mean?" I asked. "You go to the dentist like clockwork, every six months."

"I know. That will be in February."

"So?"

"I don't expect I'll be around by then."

I started to object, then stopped myself. "Do you really think so, Mother?"

"Yes," she said firmly, "I do."

"And you're trying to get prepared?"

"As best I can."

"I know it's hard."

She put on her sunglasses and changed the subject.

The next day, however, that person, the one that could make sensible plans in the face of calamity, the Mother who had been the stable center not only for her children, but for her sisters and brothers, had disappeared again. When I made my usual call that morning, I asked her how my father was doing. He had been having some pain in the aftermath of his heart surgery. "Better, I hope."

"I don't know," she answered. "I haven't seen him this morning."

I laughed uncertainly. "But surely he fixed your breakfast like always, didn't he?"

"No," she said. "It was one of those men who work around here."

Later that afternoon I went to stay with her while my father made a trip to the grocery store. She began her customary recitation of what she'd been doing that morning, as if to fix it in her own memory. Suddenly, midway through a sentence, her speech didn't make sense any more. The sounds broke apart into disconnected phrases or single words.

"I had these papers to sort . . . those long pans of food . . . what they ate."

She stopped, realizing something was askew. "I can't think of what I was going to say," she said, sounding as surprised as I felt. She lifted a thin hand and extended it, the fingers unfurling in a small gesture of futility. Or was it resignation? Shame? Patience? After a moment she replaced her hands carefully in her lap and sat very still.

I reached and touched her knee.

After another moment she looked up at me, her eyes brighter now. "Did I tell you your daddy had a twin?"

I shook my head.

"He was here at breakfast. He said he was from . . ." She paused and formed the words carefully, "Willow Creek."

"Really?"

"Yes. And he's been everywhere your father has. He even knows the same people." She peered at me closely. "Isn't that amazing?"

I raised an eyebrow and inclined my head at an angle meant to indicate tentative agreement.

She shook her head and looked away. "It was the strangest thing." Her forehead puckered momentarily. "You see there were two men," she held up two fingers, "but only one person." She shook her head again and fixed me with an intent gaze as if wanting to impart an important but difficult concept, like the Trinity. "Two men, but one person."

The pressure inside my eyes continued to hover around 18 in the right and 16 in the left. Within the normal range, Dr. H said.

"But my vision seems to be getting a little worse," I reported. "Why is that?"

"This damage is probably residual. Just now showing up from previous pressure. It takes a while." He frowned. "We'll do a CT scan. There's always the possibility of a small, benign tumor on the optic nerve."

I didn't find this answer very comforting. "I'm a writer," I told him. "I can't afford to lose my sight."

Dr. H drew himself up and began putting away his instruments. "*Everyone's* vision is important to them," he said stiffly. "I'm sure a ditch digger values his eyes as much as you."

He stood and handed me the prescription sheet with the order for the CT scan, obviously signaling the end of my appointment.

"So should I be alarmed?" I asked as I took it.

"Not alarmed," he said. "Let's say concerned."

I have no memory of the CT scan, though I can see from an old insurance billing that it was done at our local hospital.

I do remember, however, that sometime during that same summer I found Ella, a woman who could come to my parents' house every other day, take care of their housekeeping, and cook enough to carry them over the intervening day till she came again.

My mother's sister, a retired RN, was urging me to check out nursing homes in the area. But Ella, I thought, was a much better solution. She must have been around my age, as tall as my mother had once been, thin with the weary skin that bespoke a lifelong smoker. She was kind, patient, and never saw my mother as anything less than a person. Ella would sit and listen sympathetically as my mother told stories of a real past and a fantasy present. Ella could even coax her to take a bath.

When I got my mother her wheelchair, my father sobbed as he helped me unload it from the trunk of their big Crown Victoria. At first, my mother refused to use it except when I took her shopping. We wheeled up and down the aisles of Wal-Mart, a clutch of blue plastic bags hanging from the handlebars. Department stores were more difficult to navigate, especially when Christmas merchandise began to cram the aisles. Nevertheless, we managed to buy gifts for everyone, including her five great-grandchildren.

The holidays, however, were a disaster. Having visitors in the house sucked my mother into a vortex of uncontrollable hysteria on Christmas Day. I had to lead her off to the bedroom, wailing and crying. My brother and I managed to give her a sleeping pill that knocked her out until the guests were all gone.

Ella had taken the week off to be with her own family during the holidays. But in the first week of the new year, Ella's daughter called to say her mother was very ill. Another month went by before an examination at a Galveston hospital showed that Ella's old cancer had recurred. She never came back. A week before Easter, Ella died.

Meanwhile, Dr. H had still not made up his mind what exactly was ruining my vision, though I had been seeing him for almost a year.

All through the winter my sight had eroded. "If I don't get some help soon, I won't be able to drive," I told David. "I think I need another opinion."

Two weeks later I was at the Texas Medical Center in Houston, listening to a specialist in blue pajamas, young enough to be my son. He rubbed his stubble chin. "It may be glaucoma, but your field-of-vision test doesn't show a typical loss pattern for that. Usually, glaucoma loss begins on the periphery, not in your central vision. A tiny tumor that the CT scan couldn't find could be hiding back there."

But an MRI failed to find any tumor either.

"Tell you what," he finally said, "I'm going to take you down the hall to see this guy we call our glaucoma guru. I'm stumped myself."

The guru, Dr. F, was, at most, five years older than the first doctor. Like him, he was yuppie-lean, though his pajamas were green. He bounded from one examining room to another, calling orders over his shoulder to his acolytes, a string of interns and case managers. He scanned my chart, pushing back his red-gold ringlets in quick, edgy movements. Then he flashed me a quick smile, wheeled a stool up to my chair, and started with the bright-lights-in-the-eyes routine, murmuring to himself.

I held my breath, waiting for the guru's verdict. "Let's do another visual field test," he said to his assistant. "I need a baseline."

Optometrists often give this test as part of their normal screening. You put your head inside a stocklike device and stare straight ahead at the inner surface of a perfectly white globe. The attendant hands you a cord with a button to push every time you think you see a flash of light. Some of the flashes are bright, some are so dim that you're not sure whether you've actually seen them or only imagined them. And while you're trying to decide about that one, another light flashes. Your anxiety level begins to rise. You're trying to catch up on the number of flashes, but while you're trying to catch up, pinpricks of light flash elsewhere. You feel hopelessly confused, certain you've spoiled the test. The test designer, of course, has planned it this way and has built in statistical margins to compensate for your uncertainty and frustration.

When I'm done, the technician hands me the printout to take down the hall to Dr. F. The diagram shows a black patch covering about a third of the right eye's field, the central section. Another third is gray. The left eye, fortunately, shows more white space.

When Dr. F saw the results, he raised an eyebrow. "Okay," he said. "Let's do an NFA."

The nerve fiber analysis is less stressful than the field-of-vision test, and the results look much more exciting—garish red, yellow, orange, and blue splotches of something I take to represent my optic nerves. I carried the pictures back to Dr. F's warren of exam rooms and handed them over to his assistant.

Dr. F suddenly materialized, looking over his shoulder. Without a word he plucked the page from his assistant's fingers and, holding the door open to the exam room, said, "Step in here, please. Did your husband come? Good. Let's have him in too."

He didn't say any more until we were both seated, me in the examining chair with the swing-away headstock, and David in a plastic chair in a shadowy corner. The only light came from a desk lamp beside me.

"I have some news for you that, mm, isn't going to sound good."

The words didn't register at first. I was expecting to hear a diagnosis, not "news."

"You have glaucoma, all right. The problem is, it's already so advanced that it's almost too late to treat it."

The assistant opened the door and said softly, "It's Regier. He wants to know—" But Dr. F was already out the door.

David and I sat in the near darkness, neither of us saying anything for a time. I wasn't even certain I'd heard the doctor correctly.

A few minutes later Dr. F was back. "Sorry about that. Now then, where were we?" He sat down at the desk and pulled the gaudy pictures toward him. "This test shows," he began, "that you've already lost 95 percent of the right nerve and, hmm, say 85 percent of the left."

I sat there a moment without breathing. Then I said, "So that means I've only got 5 percent of my right one left and 15 percent of the left?"

He jerked his head to one side in a gesture of tentative agreement. "Round numbers," he said.

"But . . . ," I paused, "how is that possible? If I've only got 5 percent left . . . "

"How can she see as well as she does?" David interjected.

Dr. F looked faintly relieved to hear a question he could actually answer. "Redundancy," he said immediately. "The retina has so many receptors that ordinarily you can get by even if a lot of them quit working."

"But 5 percent," I repeated, still incredulous.

"Of course, there's a limit," he said, pointing to the printout of the visual field test. "As you can see, there are areas where nothing's working any more." He pointed to the black islands on the page. David left his chair in the corner and bent over the counter, peering at the test results.

When Dr. F spoke again, I could hear the gears shift in his voice. "Now then. What we have to do is treat this very aggressively in order to save what little you've got left."

I nodded, still numb.

He pulled out a shallow drawer under the counter and took out three tiny plastic bottles. "I'm giving you three different kinds of drops. This one," he said, holding up a clear plastic bottle the size of his thumbnail, "may make your eyes turn brown and will probably make your eyelashes grow thicker and longer. That'll be a permanent change." He rushed on. "You may not be able to tolerate them all, but I'm throwing everything I've got at the problem, hoping that one of these or some combination will work."

"But I've been using drops all along. What happened?"

Dr. F shrugged. "The medication tends to drift," he said.

"Drift?" I repeated.

"They can lose their effectiveness over time."

The hospital where Dr. F sees patients, does surgery, and teaches classes takes up two city blocks. The parking garages are labyrinthine. David and I wandered in a daze, trying to find our car again. We didn't say much till we were on the way home. I felt like I had a concussion.

David kept glancing at me nervously, as if waiting for me to begin.

"I know it's going to hit me after while," I said, "but just now all I feel is really angry about that word 'drift.' I mean, why be so damned poetic about it? Why can't they just say the medicine can stop working?" I rummaged in my purse for toll fares. "And why didn't anyone mention that possibility before?"

One of the three new drops felt like sandpaper in my eyes and I had to leave it off. But my intraocular pressure had fallen to 14 and 15 the following week. Dr. F beamed. "Actually, I hadn't expected the drops to work at all. I thought we'd be scheduling surgery instead." He scribbled on his prescription pad. "But it looks like this ought to hold you for at least six months."

Six months? I took a deep breath and asked matter-of-factly. "And after that?" I had learned that, if you want the straight scoop from doctors, you can't show signs of panic.

He patted my shoulder before he bolted for the door. "We'll cross that bridge when we come to it."

It wasn't a bridge I particularly wanted to cross. I was much more interested in crossing the Atlantic the following week. David and I had planned our first vacation since moving back to Texas—two weeks in England. My immediate worries about my eyes relieved, I focused on reading guidebooks. Somehow I entirely forgot Dr. F's six-month timeline.

We were in Cambridge, just leaving Kings College after hearing evensong one afternoon when I caught hold of David's arm.

"Has the weather suddenly turned stormy?" I asked him.

"No. Why?"

"You're sure it's not cloudy? It just seems darker all of a sudden."

He stared at me, then put his hand over mine. "Watch your step," he said.

The evening before we flew home, we ate outdoors at the Six Bells, a fifteenth-century pub beside the Mole River. Eight years earlier, in what now seemed another life, my mother and I had eaten lunch there. I had asked her if she were ready to go home, now that our trip was drawing to a close.

"No," she'd sighed, watching blossoms from a lime tree float down to the meandering water's surface. "I'd like this to go on forever."

That's how I felt now. I didn't want to hear what Dr. F would tell me when I got back.

Three weeks later I'm lying on a gurney in the prep area outside the operating room of the Medical Center while the resident on duty that day, a Turkish anesthesiologist named Dr. A, explains that he needs to know how much I weigh so he can measure the amount of nerve-blocker to inject in my arm.

Dr. F flies past my gurney. "So how are you?"

"Cold."

"We can fix that," he says with exaggerated cheer and takes a blanket—my third—from a warming cabinet.

Dr. F always acts as if he's the host at a party, flitting from guest to guest, keeping the tone upbeat, wanting everyone to be happy, while at the same time never forgetting that he is, after all, the host and that this is his party.

I start to ask him a question—I have hundreds—but already the gurney is moving and a clear plastic mask is being fitted over my face. Someone clamps a speculum to my right eye to hold the lid open.

I already know from quizzing Dr. A that I will be awake, more or less, during the operation—a trabulectomy, which Dr. F reduces with insider's insouciance to "trab."

"I can't see through this microscope," an intern to my right complains.

Behind my head I hear the voice of Dr. F. "That's the new one. What's wrong? Can't you focus it?"

His apprentice replies with a trace of petulance, "It's not a question of focusing. I can't see anything at all."

"Mine's working fine," Dr. F says, "And it's twenty-five years old. Hand me a super-sharp."

I wince.

Dr. F: "Can you mop up here? I can't see. The blood's getting in my way."

I feel something brush my cheek.

Dr. F again: "I need a spoon. Hand me a spoon."

"A spoon!" I blurt out suddenly. "You're doing this with a spoon?"

"Just one of the instruments," Dr. F says shortly. "You'll have to keep quiet so I can concentrate."

I try to keep quiet but not drift into sleep from the sedative Dr. A gave me. I listen to the snip of the scissors, the comments Dr. F makes to his student and the nurse about the size of the "plug" he's removing. My heart, chirping steadily on the monitor, speeds up for a couple of beats when I inhale, then slows till I release my breath.

Dr. F at last heaves a sigh and says to his intern, "Okay. You want to close?"

"Sure. My microscope's working now."

"Yeah, I see. It was unplugged. Didn't you notice? Use 30-gauge to close."

As soon as Dr. F is out of the room, I start quizzing the young intern. "How can you sew an eyeball? Isn't it like trying to sew Jell-O?"

"You don't sew the eyeball itself," he says. The vitreous has skin over it—a membrane. That's what I'm stitching."

I listen to the clip of his scissors, feel the tug of the 30-gauge whatever, wonder if the number means the same as the measure of fishing line. But I don't ask, not wanting to distract him. When he's through, I ask, "How many stitches did it take?"

"Well," he begins, sounding half earnest, half defensive, "we do a running stitch, so I guess it's technically just one."

"Sort of like basting."

It's obvious from the ensuing silence that he probably thinks I'm talking about turkeys.

Dr. A, so silent I have not been sure if he were still there, removes the IV needle from my arm, looks up at the clock, and says, "Forty-five. No, forty-six minutes."

Do they charge by the minute for the operating room? Or do they place bets on the day's best time?

As the nurse tapes a bulging metal shield over my eye, Dr. F starts rattling off instructions to me. "Leave the shield on overnight. I'll remove it tomorrow. You shouldn't feel much pain, but you can take Tylenol if you need to. No bending, lifting, or straining. I'll give you different drops to take tomorrow. Let's see . . . what time?"

He snatches the receiver off the wall phone and punches in a number. "When's my flight in the morning? Okay." He hangs up and says, "Seven-thirty. Upstairs. You're going to be fine."

And, as a matter of fact, I was. "Textbook," Dr. F said on the post-op visit.

But how long will this fix last? I want to know the odds. When I asked Dr. F what I should expect five years from now, he said without blinking, "I have no idea."

Facts about blindness, I'm learning, can turn as slippery as those about the brain. The odds elude calculation. Those, like me, with end-stage glaucoma, don't slide down a gradual incline into darkness. Instead they drop over the edge of a series of plateaus. Not until I have a low vision evaluation a year later does the examiner tell me I could wake up one morning with all my sight having drained away overnight.

"Not that any of the doctors here will tell you that," she said, handing me a catalogue for "assistive technology" products. "But I'd be surprised if you made it five more years."

Like most people, I had always imagined blindness as a dark room, complete blackness. But eighty percent of the legally blind have some vision, even if it's only perception of light and darkness. Blindness comes in many guises. Some people lose their central vision first. In others, the periphery of the visual field is gradually whittled away. To qualify as blind for tax exemptions or federal assistance programs, a doctor must certify that you have:

1. not more than 20/200 central visual acuity in the better eye with correcting lenses, or
2. a limitation to the field of vision in the better eye to such

a degree that its widest diameter subtends an angle of no greater than twenty degrees.

The gradual death of my optic nerve cells has left blank patches on my retina. Those areas perceive nothing at all. Not blackness, just nothing.

The brain soon learns to compensate for aberrant visual input. In a carnival fun house you may feel off balance by the optical illusions designed to trick your brain. But given time, your brain would sort the distorted visual information and make sense of it. My brain, for instance, fills in the blank spots with what I can best describe as smears. This ruse works fairly well, though later, I would discover, not well enough for certain activities. Reading, for instance. And driving.

I quickly learned what dependency feels like. Negotiating elevators, steps, doorways the day after surgery, I grabbed for David's arm. I wanted him always near me, within reach. Otherwise I felt panicky, adrift. After a few weeks I could sense how effortlessly I could slip into treating him as an extension of my own body, making his hands, feet, eyes, my own. I could easily learn to take for granted his unflagging attention, just as I expect my own hands and feet to respond automatically to my needs. And also to know instantly when I don't want help. This, I could tell, was going to be a delicate balancing act.

For David, I became some strange fusion of treasure and burden. I had to be protected, cared for, maneuvered. For his part, he sometimes expected me to be as acquiescent as a suitcase. I didn't blame him. I've been taking care of my mother; I understand how impatient one becomes when trying to get someone across a busy street, for instance, when the person wants you to explain every move. It's a dance we both have to learn. How to keep from being too demanding, too dependent, too arbitrary. The same minuet I've done with my mother. Only now the tables are turned.

The summer after my first surgery, I talked with Lola, my mother's ninety-year-old cousin who was rapidly going blind from macular degeneration. "My granddaughter," Lola tells me in a confidential undertone, "was terribly upset when she heard my diagnosis. Crying and carrying on." Lola shakes her head. "Finally I said, 'Okay, young lady, we're a-going to talk about it this one time." Lola wags her forefinger, reenacting the confrontation. "And then I don't want to hear no more about it."

I don't spend much time thinking about going blind and, like Lola, I enjoy talking about it even less. When I do think about it, the opening line from Milton's sonnet on his blindness best captures my thoughts. When I consider how my light is spent . . . . How to spend the light I've got left—that's what concerns me most these days.

Arthur Frank, in his book *The Wounded Storyteller*, tells of a woman who successfully recovered from a cerebral aneurysm, though one side remained weak and she experienced occasional double vision that such a stroke often leaves behind. The woman referred to her condition as her "ethnicity."

The late Mark O'Brien was a writer who went to classes at the University of California at Berkeley on an electric gurney that he propelled by using one of the four muscles still functioning in his body. "Saying a disabled person is courageous," he wrote, "is like saying that a black person has natural rhythm."

I find myself agreeing with both these comments. I now belong to that ethnic mouthful, the "visually impaired." A caseworker, in the midst of giving me information about disability programs, suddenly turned red with embarrassment. "Not that you're disabled," he stammered. "I mean, there's not anything *wrong* with you."

"Listen," I said, "obviously something is very wrong with me. Not being able to see is definitely disabling. Don't worry. The truth doesn't offend me."

On the other hand, like Mark O'Brien, I am offended when certain virtues are automatically attributed to me. Courage doesn't automatically accompany blindness. Some paraplegics are brave; some are whiners. The same is true of blind people. And most of the time, like Lola, they'd rather talk about something else.

I thought at first what I would miss most was not being able to read. But I was an easy convert to the Library of Congress's Talking Books program. Words, after all, are essentially voice, not marks. I now prefer taking in books through my ears instead of my eyes. Perhaps this was an early, if unwitting, gift from my mother, who read to me every night at bedtime when I was a child.

My greatest loss has not been of words, but of landscape. The detail of outdoors. Crisp horizons, leaf veins, concentrated color. I still prefer the real world to look like Wyeth rather than Renoir.

My friend Lee tells me I am living her worst nightmare. But I can think of far worse hardships. My mother's, for instance. I may be losing my sight, but she's losing her self. Some parts of us are more expendable than others.

Better, I tell my friend, paraphrasing Scripture, I should enter life with one eye than with two eyes to be thrown into the hell of dementia.

7
The Crash

When I was a child, my mother always made a fuss over birthdays. The honoree got not just gifts but special attention all day, including favorite foods at dinner. After I left home I could always count on packages in the mail and a phone call from home.

But on my fifty-eighth birthday, when I made what had become my regular morning phone call to my parents, neither seemed aware there was anything special about the day. My father only mentioned "a little fall" my mother had had that morning

"Nothing much really," he said.

My mother had been falling a lot lately. Just a week earlier, as I was coming through their front gate, I saw the two of them making their way along the lane where they take their evening walks.

I raised my hand to wave, and at that instant my mother toppled over onto her right side like a puppet whose strings had suddenly been cut.

For an instant time stopped flowing and turned instead into a series of discrete still photographs. In the first, she is falling, the hem of her pink and blue dress flaring slightly behind her.

In the next flash, her arms are spread wide and her walking stick is suspended in midair, while my father's face registers something like puzzlement.

The camera clicks again, and I see him crumpled to his knees beside her.

All this happens in a moment, and then time starts to move again while I am trying to inhale and at the same time to shout.

"Don't move! Are you all right?"

When I reach them, my mother is looking dazed and my father is already assuming an air of calm, if defensive, control. She sits up and points to her glasses which have skidded across the driveway. I retrieve them, and we go inside, get her a glass of water, maneuver our way through their mutual embarrassment.

Not many days later my mother fell again, this time while trying to carry some cups into the kitchen. I was not there at the time. I took my parents' word for it that she had suffered no damage in the fall other than a scraped hand.

So on this birthday morning when my father mentions "a little fall," I figure it is probably on a par with these earlier ones and that I can check it out later before I leave for an appointment with my own doctor.

I stop by around one o'clock. My mother is in bed and her cousin Margaret is trying to cajole her into eating the lunch on the tray beside her. Margaret looks at me across the room, letting me know she is worried. I say I'll be back as quickly as I can.

At 3:30, I find my mother still dazed and frightened. When Margaret and I try to maneuver her onto the potty-chair beside her bed, I discover she isn't able to move her legs. In fact, she didn't seem to understand when I tell her to put her arms around my waist so I can make the transfer. I nearly drop her when her muscles lock tight.

I stand back from the bed and take a deep breath, trying to hide my own panic. Margaret stares at me hard.

"This is dangerous," I say.

She nods.

I go to the phone in the living room and call my mother's family doctor who tells me to take her to the hospital where he will meet us in the emergency room.

Somehow, between my father, Margaret, and me, we manage to get my mother into her wheelchair.

As I maneuver it through the bedroom door and up the hallway, neither wide enough for easy access, my mother's eyes are wide with fright. She catches at the doorframe. Gently I loosen her fingers.

"We have to go to the hospital now, Mother." I whisper the words so my voice won't break. This could be, I know, the last time she sees her home. Resolutely I stuff the thought into a dark corner of my mind.

An hour later, while my mother is being x-rayed and CT-scanned, David and I have a quick supper at the Burger King down the street from the hospital. My father has refused to leave the emergency waiting room.

"Happy birthday," David says, raising his plastic cup to toast the occasion. "What a birthday present, huh?"

I shrug and stare off into the kiddy playroom where a couple of preschoolers are scooping up armloads of plastic balls and throwing them over their heads.

My mother had brought up the subject of a nursing home several weeks earlier. We were sitting on her front porch in the late afternoon. She was more coherent than she had been for a while.

"I'm getting worse," she said.

I held my breath, not wanting to contradict this or change the subject. For some time I had seen that she needed more nursing care than my father and I could provide. She already had to be lifted out of her chair, have her medications closely monitored, had to be bathed and toileted.

I kept quiet and waited for her to continue.

"I guess I'll have to go . . . ," she hesitated, searching for some word that she could both pronounce and bear, "to a facility."

I drew in a long, slow breath. Was she just trying out how this sounded, expecting me to protest?

"Which one do you prefer?" I asked.

Her hand groped toward her head and then fell into her lap again. "The one where Curtis is, I guess."

"Curtis?" It took me a moment to remember their friend at church. "You mean Curtis Hardesty?"

"Yes," she said. "He's been there about three years now. Not knowing anything."

I said nothing. I didn't know anything either.

When I had reported to my father that my mother was talking about a nursing home, he was horrified. He shook his head and turned away.

My mother's sister, a nurse whose own husband had died after a seven-year decline with Parkinson's, had long been urging me to look into nursing home care for my mother.

"I had help from Medicare to cover home health care for Roy," she told me. "That's how I could keep him at home. But Medicare doesn't do that any longer."

When relatives asked my mother about her condition she always insisted she was "fine."

"And I'm fine too," my father would say in a quavery voice. "We're making it. They're not going to take her away from me."

"They," of course, meant me.

"She's my mate," he would protest, as if they were a pair of snow geese. It was a term he had often used for my mother, one she didn't particularly like.

"I've taken a vow to keep her right here at home," he would declare, his voice breaking, "as long as God gives me breath."

It's hard to remember now how angry that ultimatum made me then. Not only did it seem a veiled accusation, but it showed how little my father was aware of the support troops who made it possible to keep my mother at home. Friends and relatives drove my father to his out-of-town medical appointments, mowed their three-acre lawn, fixed broken plumbing, brought casseroles and cakes, painted their porch, stayed with my mother when Margaret or I were out of town. All of these people, many in their seventies, had been working to sustain my parents' illusion of independence.

I could feel the heat of an old anger and stubbornness rise in my blood. Replaying our ancient quarrels, I knew, would give me no joy and only turn my mother into a pawn. So I had dropped the subject of a nursing home.

Nothing more was said about a nursing home for a while. The following week I had taken her for a liver function test the neurologist had ordered. Afterward, as I was helping her undress at home, she gave a feeble kick at the slippers I had just pulled off her feet.

"You can just throw those away," she said crossly.

I sat beside her on the bed, staring at the slippers. They were new and expensive. They were the third pair she had rejected, each discarded when she insisted they were responsible for her falls. And when it wasn't the shoes tripping her up, it was the "mud seeping up through the carpet."

I sat there holding the slipper in my hand and feeling my throat constrict to hold back a wail.

"Mother," I said, "I'm at the end of my rope."

She stared at me.

I swallowed. "I just don't know what to do next."

The silence continued. Those plain, hard words tasted like salt and vinegar on my tongue.

"You and Pop both are in such denial about your situation," I stopped and shook my head. "I guess we'll just wait till the next crisis." Then I picked up the offending slippers, set them neatly in her closet, and went home.

The next day both my parents were like eager puppies, tumbling over themselves in their effort to appease me. I took entirely too much pleasure in this reaction to my words. I wanted to be kind and patient, not smug and vindictive.

Competing voices haunted the darkness as I lay sleepless at night. One whispered, Which is more important—my mother's safety or her freedom to choose? But then another voice countered with a second question: Is my mother choosing or is my father choosing for her? And which part of my mother's fractured identity was speaking for her truest self?

I was clear about what I wanted, however. I wanted my

mother in a nursing home. So she'd be safe. So I wouldn't have to worry constantly about her falling. So it wouldn't be my fault if she did. So I could get some sleep.

Her own choice had vacillated from day to day. More days than not, she wanted to remain at home. But her fears about intruders had not abated. Only rarely was she as clearheaded about her situation as she had been that afternoon on the porch when she first raised the subject. On the other hand, how responsible was it to allow the part of her that was least in touch with reality to do the choosing?

I was stymied.

Until that moment, sitting in the Burger King booth with David. I crumpled the greasy hamburger wrapper into a tight orange ball.

"I guess I got my birthday wish," I said to David. "I don't think she's going back home this time."

Pushing open the door to the hospital waiting room again, I knew we had reached a turning point. And an hour later, when the doctor confirmed that my mother had suffered a hemorrhagic stroke, I was all but certain she would not be going home again.

After my mother was moved out of the intensive care unit and to the recovery ward, I went numbly about the business of dealing with doctors, nursing staff, and relatives. They all seemed like stick figures, not quite real. In fact, nothing seemed quite real. I felt as if I'd landed on an alien planet where I was forced to communicate with the natives in a strange, truncated trade language. "How! Me daughter. You doctor."

Anger was the only emotion I could access. Not grief, not fear. Just a generalized, almost uncontrollable anger. I tried not to answer the phone, but when I was forced to take calls from concerned friends and relatives, I felt like shouting, "Leave me alone. Go find your own tragedy. This one's taken!"

My aunt, the nurse, arrived at the hospital. "I'll have supper ready for you when you get home," she promised my father as she left.

At ten-thirty that evening, she called me at home. "Have you seen your dad?" she asked. "He hasn't come home yet."

"I'll call Mother's room," I told her.

The phone rang a dozen times, but no one answered. David drove to the hospital and found him sound asleep on a cot in my mother's room.

I was at the hospital by 7:30 the next morning. "We had no idea what had happened to you last night," I told him. "Why didn't you let us know where you were?"

He pointed to his ear and shrugged. "Guess I couldn't hear the phone. I had my hearing aid out. You could have called the nurses' station. They could have told you I was here."

I sent him home, then sat and watched my mother breathe. She hadn't waked when I came in or when my father left. My aunt had told me there was a chance she might have another stroke soon. One often follows on the heels of the first, like aftershocks from earthquakes.

I grew panicky when her breathing would slow. What seemed like minutes would creep by before I saw her chest lift slightly again.

At ten, I called David at his office. "She still hasn't waked up," I told him. "Not even when the nurse came in with her medication."

"Well, if the nurse has seen her . . ."

"What if they want to put her on life support? I forgot to bring her living will with me."

"It's all right," he said. "She's going to be all right."

No, I thought, she's never going to be all right. Not in this world.

David, for all his calm reassurance, came home shaken that evening. He had stopped by the hospital to see my mother after his last class and found her crying, her talk full of guilt and fear that she might be abandoned.

"It was all I could do to leave her like that," he said.

I stood at the stove, silently stirring soup.

"Maybe you should go back up there tonight," he suggested.

I wiped the countertop, reached into the cabinet for plates.

Finally I said, "After supper I'll call the hospital and ask the charge nurse how she's doing."

Wilma, the charge nurse, had, as it turned out, worked with my mother years before. She laughed when I asked about my mother.

"Lord, honey, she had the biggest old bowel movement this evening you ever saw. And two different men come to see her. I reckon they must have been from her church. I sat and drank coffee with her while she ate her supper. We chatted about old times at the office."

Wilma, I imagined, must have done most of the chatting. It was hard to picture my mother chatting, when she could, only with great difficulty and not much volume, manage a few words at a time.

That night I had an appalling dream in which my mother was trying to kill me. We were both in a cavernous barn, she up in the hayloft, throwing chunks of concrete down at me. The scene shifted to an arena with tiered bleachers. She took a seat several rows behind me, but kept stretching to reach me with the obvious intention of strangling me. Then suddenly another shadowy figure was beside me, trying to help me. Neither of us fought back; we simply tried to avoid my mother's grasp. Strangely, she did not seem angry, only determined to kill me. She was much younger in the dream, around forty or so. And I too was younger. So was my obscure helper. I worried that my mother might give up trying to strangle me and simply shoot me. Eventually she left the arena and when she returned, she took a seat in a row below and in front of me and my unknown helper. She had changed her blouse to one that was black with flowers on it. Still, she wasn't enraged or ranting, just inexorable. Nor was I angry. Just scared out of my wits.

The dream is pretty transparent, I realize. And when I woke up, what bothered me most was not being able to identify the person who had helped me. Was it, I hardly dared hope, the same shrouded figure who had walked alongside the two disheartened disciples on the road to Emmaus?

8

The Nursing Home

Some decisions you make by plunging—from a riverbank, a cliff's edge, a rooftop. Once the die is cast, there's no turning back. Other decisions are retrievable. You can reconsider, change your mind, do it over. On the face of it, this second kind is preferable. Such decisions are not final; we all like second chances.

But a decision you can revoke also has its drawbacks. It can make you lie awake at night, the voice inside your head laying out evidence for and against, going round and round the rut it has already worn in your brain.

That's how it was after my mother's stroke, when the time finally came to move her from the transitional care unit at the hospital to the nursing home. Some nights that's how it still is.

My father was not a decisive person. Throughout my parents' fifty-eight years together, my mother had been the default and de facto decision maker. Now that task became mine. In fact, several years before my mother's illness, both my parents had begun turning to me to make some decisions for them.

When it was time to decide about the nursing home, I knew how the process would play out. After my mother's time in rehab was up, the doctor would ask what we wanted to do next. My father would turn and look at me, pulling thoughtfully on the fleshy wattle under his chin. If I tried to outwait him, he would give a little shrug of his shoulders and stare down at his hands. If the doctor then laid out the alternatives—back to the house or to the nursing home—my father would begin to cry. The doctor would turn to me a little impatiently, waiting for an answer.

From the beginning I had seen this hospitalization as something of a godsend. We had gone through half a dozen helpers I hired through a private home health care agency. Some had been better than others; none, however, would be able to cope with my mother alone now. It took two people to lift her from bed to wheelchair or potty-chair, or—terrifying thought—into the tub. My father wasn't strong enough to be one of those people. Nor could he hear when she called. He often took extravagant risks trying to please her or satisfy clearly irrational demands she made.

But without the crisis of my mother's last stroke, my father would never have even considered Fair Acres as an alternative. An indecisive person can also be stubborn. Until this last crisis, coercion would have required more resolve or arbitrary force than I could bring myself to exert. But now my mother's two-week hospital stay had provided the necessary bridge to the nursing home. The time had come to cross the bridge I had so long dreaded.

Her stroke had sent my mother to the hospital on my birthday. We moved her to Fair Acres on David's birthday. I made my way through that day, talking with doctors, nurses, therapists, and administrators, using the part of my brain that handles crises. The people I was dealing with probably thought I was sane, reasonably calm, and in control of my emotions. But having to act while being of two minds means the self is unsteady, off balance, tottering on the brink of dissolution. The clinical term, I believe, is dissociation.

Driving home from the nursing home that first day, I couldn't figure out what season of the year we were in. I'd been

writing the date on admitting papers all day, but I was shocked
to see dogwood in bloom along the roadside, azaleas covered
with fuchsia blossoms, and wisteria drooping with heavy clus-
ters of lavender. I had somehow expected red and yellow leaves
to be drifting down from the trees instead. How could it be
spring? I felt as if I had just landed on the planet after a long
absence, uncertain where the sun was in its circuit.

That night, the case for my mother's move, whose outcome
had seemed foregone during the daylight hours, began its
relentless recapitulation in my head. Why couldn't we care for
my mother at home?

In a word—money. My mother needed round-the-clock
nursing care now. Medicare does not cover visits from home
health care workers for patients like my mother who have a
degenerative disease such as Parkinson's or Alzheimer's. Nor did
she qualify for hospice care. To receive those benefits, the
attending physician must certify that the patient has, by a reasonable estimate, no more than six months to live. No one
knew how much longer my mother might live. Round-the-
clock private care at home would cost between six and ten thousand dollars a month. And that was supposing we could find
skilled people who would show up day after day.

But couldn't I do it myself, bring her back to my house?
Lying there in bed, I would contract my muscles, as if testing
whether I had the physical strength to carry out the number of
transfers—bed, chair, bath, toilet—that would be necessary
during an average day. I doubted it. My mother, in the good old
days, had been almost six feet tall. Even with her dwindling
weight, she weighed more than me.

But hospital nurses my size handle patients larger than themselves every day. If they could do it, surely I could learn their
technique. Maybe. Again, I doubted it. In addition to her size,
my mother's frozen muscles and joints were another obstacle.
Lifting her was like trying to dance with a bicycle. Which is why
it took two skilled aides to carry out the task.

Also, neither my house nor my parents' was wheelchair-
accessible. We might build ramps outside, but the hallways and

varying floor levels would make it difficult even to move her from room to room.

Despite this nightly debate in my brain, the most difficult question came to this: How can you tell your mother, "This is where you belong," when you know she wouldn't be there if she had any choice in the matter? For my mother, clearly, did not now want to be in a nursing home, no matter what she had said to me in earlier months. Nor did 95 percent of the other residents at Fair Acres, I eventually realized.

You can feel it as soon as you come in the door. Cold rage. For most of the people parked in wheelchairs, their anger has gone so stale after years of overuse that the emotion is routine now. Sometimes it modulates to mere resentment or apathy. Always, however, it accuses. Anyone is culpable who comes through the front doors and is free to leave again under their own steam.

And who can blame these judges? Two-thirds of people in nursing homes have no regular visitors. No one chooses to live there because they like it. Like my mother, they have no better option available. Almost always, someone else has made this choice for them.

Nor should the able-bodied expect any mitigation of their verdict. These judges do not recognize degrees of suffering. None of them looks around and sees that other residents may be worse off. In fact, only rarely does one resident even acknowledge the existence of another.

During those first weeks in Fair Acres, I sat watching group exercise sessions from the sidelines, hoping my mother would make a friend among the other residents—whom she called "inmates." When the activity director coaxed the residents to play games, they came as close as they ever did to acknowledging one another's existence. But my mother pitched beanbag frogs at plastic lily pads as if this too were a test she expected to fail.

Surely, I thought, she would eventually form a bond with some other woman, perhaps at her table in the dining room. But no. She hated going to the dining room. Like many of the other residents, she ate quite slowly. Her tablemates, she told me, made fun of her, even hated her.

I was shocked. Despite her natural reserve, even shyness, my mother had always considered it something of a moral obligation to make friends, to be, as she put it, sociable. Indeed, next to her children, my mother's many friends had proved one of her chief pleasures in life. She kept up with their birthdays, wrote them notes, made phone calls, invited them to visit. Her sympathies with their difficulties ran deep. Several times during the past year, despite her worsening condition, I had taken her to visit friends who were homebound or in the hospital. Not only did she consider this her Christian duty, but she enjoyed seeing them. Yet now she made no effort to connect with anyone else at Fair Acres.

During those first days and weeks in the nursing home, I would wheel my mother to her table in the dining room, my face set in a plaintive smile. "Speak, Mother," I would urge under my breath when one of her tablemates ventured a comment. But the look my mother turned on me mingled outrage, dismay, and shock. She did not speak.

Nor did she cooperate with the physical therapist, a tiny young woman who tried to get her to stack blocks, string large plastic rings on a rope, propel her own wheelchair. My mother would fumble with the blocks a few minutes, then shake her head and indicate she was too tired to continue. If the therapist tried to push on, my father, who insisted on attending these sessions, grew angry and defensive.

"Can't you see she's tired?" he would cry. "She's been through too much already. You don't need to torture her."

For my part, all I did, all I knew how to do, was show up every afternoon and sit beside my mother.

"You're making a mistake," a friend advised me. "Three times a week, that should be your limit. I took Aunt Irma fried chicken on Monday, grapes on Wednesday, and doughnuts on Friday. She always knew what to look forward to. Frankly, I think that's all she cared about—getting her goodies."

When I was silent, my friend added, "Of course, I know

you're a lot closer to your mother. But you're going to have to pace yourself. You have no idea how long this might last."

But I found it impossible to think of cutting back on my time with her. Or, more accurately, while I could think and consider that possibility, I couldn't act on it. The only time my mother achieved some level, not of happiness or contentment, but at least decreased anxiety, was when a family member was with her.

"What you ought to have," my experienced friend advised, "is about a two-week period of separation, when you don't go there at all. That way she'll get used to it. And she'll come to depend on the staff to help her. Sort of transfer her expectations from you to them. As long as you keep going, she'll expect you to be there all the time."

She was right. My mother never transferred an ounce of her expectations to the staff. Maybe because my father was with her every morning and evening, for lunch and supper, missing only a few days when he was sick or had inescapable appointments. Maybe too because I was with her every afternoon, sometimes spelled by Margaret so I could go to the grocery store.

At the beginning, the staff, convinced that our routine would eventually become less regular, said nothing about this arrangement. Later one of the nurses advised us to ease back, saying that my mother needed to get used to the schedule there, to adjust. But we couldn't help ourselves. It was like putting a child in foster care or an orphanage. How could we walk away, leaving her to feel totally abandoned, especially during those initial weeks?

Did my mother sense that? Did she purposely manipulate our emotions?

Of course. Even after two more strokes would further bruise her brain, some days she still cried and pleaded for us not to leave her. Wouldn't you?

Everyone has heard nursing home horror stories. My mother's unhappiness no doubt made us extra vigilant about her care at Fair Acres. We were on the alert for any sign of mistreatment or neglect. At the same time, we needed to develop a good relationship with the staff—especially the aides who had the most contact with the residents—if my mother was to get the best care there.

Nursing homes are governed, not just by rules and guidelines devised by state agencies, nor even by standard medical protocols, but by the far more subtle forces of economics and social conditions. Fair Acres was run by a nursing home corporation based in Houston. It paid aides $7.35 an hour. It would no doubt pay less except that, at the time my mother was admitted, the country was experiencing record low unemployment rates, and it was difficult to keep enough workers to satisfy even minimal standards.

The work is physically demanding and ranks about the level of garbage collector in prestige. Given a choice—and the unemployment rate—most people preferred to work for fast food franchises rather than spend their days changing adult diapers and lifting frail, demented octogenarians.

Most of the nursing aides were high school dropouts, had several children at home, and no husband. They were often pressed to work double shifts when their scheduled replacements didn't show up. Turnover is high.

The best among them move up from nursing aide to medication aide as soon as they pass the requisite course for certification. That work is both less exhausting and more prestigious. The med aide pushes a wheeled metal cabinet along the hallway, dispensing pills in tiny paper cups and recording each dose. The next stratum of the hierarchy, a "treatment" nurse, inspects cuts, bruises, incisions, and eruptions, medicating and bandaging, making sure to write the date on the tape. Both these jobs carry a certain medical cachet. Yet even so, they are still "working the halls."

Nearly all nursing homes are designed around a central hub—the nurses' station—with the patients' rooms lining hallways splayed out like legs from a spider's body. Within the circular nerve center, shielded by a chest-high counter, dwell the "charge nurses." These are usually licensed vocational nurses,

LVNs, not RNs. The latter are in such short supply they are snapped up, at higher wages, by hospitals. Though Medicare and Medicaid designated Fair Acres as a "skilled nursing facility," the only registered nurse employed there was Lorene Lightfoot, the Director of Nurses.

Of course, as an administrator, Lorene spends most of her time talking to doctors, vendors, and family members, doing paper work, training other employees. She mostly sees patients—or residents—only when company policy requires it or while passing through the halls or in the dining room.

As LVNs, the charge nurses are the institution's noncommissioned officers. They have more contact with residents. From their central bunker behind the circular desk, they can observe the ambulatory residents sitting in the parlor or making their way to the activity room and the dining room. Those parked in wheelchairs around the desk they can easily keep an eye on. But patients confined to their rooms they see only if there's a problem or a special request. One newly hired male nurse, stethoscope draped around his neck, checks on each patient when his shift begins, but that attention is rare.

Like any other cross section of human beings, some aides and nurses do a good job, some do not. Some are responsible and compassionate, others are unreliable and sullen. Among the charge nurses, some are attentive and competent, while their colleagues sit and gossip.

Only rarely do I see or speak with the director of nursing. She shares an office with the assistant director of nursing where I go with problems about my mother's care. She nods and takes notes as you tell her about your mother's dirty diaper, her need for a change in diet, the bath she didn't get that morning. After assuring you the matter will be taken care of, she passes the information on to the assistant whose responsibility it is to "visit" with you about these problems.

Generally, the assistant director of nursing is responsible for actually carrying out whatever action is deemed appropriate. Therefore, she tends to be a good bit more defensive. "We must keep our expectations realistic," she reminds you. She sometimes even edges toward hints that, should your dissatisfaction with the establishment reach too high a level, you might want to consider making other arrangements for your mother.

I try to make as few complaints as possible. In the first eighteen months, I probably talked to the director of nursing a total of four times. I also wrote a letter once to the director of Fair Acres, when my mother went for four days without a bath. He did not reply, but then I did not expect that he would. I sometimes see him running a hand through his thinning red hair as he sails, shirt-sleeved, from the administrative wing into the dining room.

He invites everyone to call him "L.V." At the facility's quarterly "Family Councils," he addresses in a hearty, booming voice the dozen or so adult children, spouses, siblings, or friends of residents sitting around the dining tables where, an hour hence, our relatives will be eating supper.

"I just wanted to spell out a few changes we've instituted," L.V. tells us. "Lula had to leave us—Clyde's retiring and they want to do some traveling." Lula has been the activity director during the previous year. Most of her energies went into decorating the halls for various holidays—not just Thanksgiving and Christmas, but St. Patrick's Day, Valentine's Day, Memorial Day. Any occasion with a theme.

"But we've got an energetic young lady who's going to be taking her place," L.V. assures us. "Heather McBride. Come on up here, Heather, and tell us about what you've got planned."

Everyone claps encouragingly for Heather, who looks to be a new graduate of the town's university, probably with a degree in something like recreation therapy. Heather tells us there's going to be movie day once a week when she'll play a classic video and serve popcorn. The oldies but goodies, she says reassuringly. The once-a-month birthday parties for the residents who've lived yet another year will continue. "I've got some ideas for music and exercise too," she adds, bouncing on her toes.

Next, L.V. tells us about the new alarm system installed for the exits at the ends of the spider-leg halls and we all clap for Arnie, the maintenance man who carried out the innovation.

Finally, the director asks for questions and comments from us, reminding us that the staff is only there to serve these loved ones of ours, adding that this, after all, is *their* home, and the staff merely their helpers.

Few people ask questions. If David is there, he usually poses one. But after the meetings he makes a point of instigating an amiable, supportive conversation with L.V. in the hall outside his office. He's good at eliciting more information that way from the director, who seems glad of the opportunity for masculine talk.

My mother, however, is not one of the residents who will be eating in the dining room later. She eats breakfast there, but takes her other meals in her room with my father. She hates the dining room. It makes her feel exposed. Since moving to the nursing home, she has had no more hallucinations about strange men coming in through the windows or sinister figures in the attic. But her paranoia now takes this new form of believing that other residents and aides ridicule her.

For my part, I have made some friends among the staff. It would be strange to go someplace every day for a year and a half and fail to form at least a few connections. I have my favorites among the aides. For a long time, Linda was at the top of the list. Built like a sumo wrestler, she wore her hair clipped as close to her skull as possible, a style that showed off the planes of her dark face to good effect. The first time I complimented her hairstyle, she was suspicious, but later, when I cautioned her about lifting my mother by herself because she might injure herself, Linda brushed my worry aside good-naturedly. "I been doing this for years now. And your mama don't weigh hardly nothing anyway."

Linda has several children at home. She often worked double shifts, after which she had to go home at eleven o'clock at night to wash clothes, clean, and cook. I fretted about her overwork; she laughed at this on some days and sighed dejectedly on others. Linda was the only aide who ever put my mother on the commode in the toilet shared with the adjoining room. That maneuver required a two-step process—transferring my mother's stiff body into her wheelchair first, then from the wheelchair onto the toilet seat. My mother much preferred this to the potty-chair that the other aides placed beside her bed so that they would only have to lift her once. I didn't protest their choice, but I was grateful to Linda for her extra effort.

Finally, Linda began to talk of quitting. "This place down in Conroe, they pay almost eight bucks an hour."

"But you'd have a thirty-mile commute, one way," I said.

"I got a friend already working down there. We can go together."

Linda's friend, Estelle, also one of my favorites, told me not to worry. "Linda ain't gonna quit. Linda's always talking like that, but she won't do it."

Linda's threats went on for a couple of months. I had pretty well discounted them, deciding Estelle was right. I kept on alternately telling Linda she was working too hard and begging her not to leave Fair Acres. But she injured her back one day, took what workman's comp she could get for a while, and then gave her two weeks' notice. Estelle assured me she'd be back. But she didn't return. What's more, two more weeks later, Estelle was gone too.

Linda was eventually replaced with Jolene, a tall, pale woman around forty whose husband had died two years previously. She has worked in nursing homes for eighteen years, she tells me. Her devotion to patients appears absolute. Still, though she never finished high school, Jolene hopes to get into the next round of training sessions for med aides.

Linda, Estelle, and Jolene are exceptional. They fill the top echelon—excellent—of the roughly four categories into which I divide nurse's aides. Next on my list come the "desirables," those who respond with reasonable promptness to the call button and who do a good job of keeping my mother clean and comfortable. They may be cheerful or matter-of-fact, but they never try to talk to my mother or make her feel that she's a person the way the best ones do. In the third level—"better than nothing"—are those who are more or less haphazard in the way they fix her bed or clean and dress her, forgetting to put socks on her always icy feet or buttoning her dress crookedly. Mercifully few aides fall into the last and worst category. These don't respond at all to the call light. I have to hunt for them in the TV room or on the patio where they go to smoke. They mutter sullenly to one another and will not answer questions or even respond when I thank them for their help.

But even when a patient is left in a dirty diaper at the end of a shift, one hesitates before complaining to the charge nurses. Within any institution, you learn to spend your credit carefully. Nursing homes are no exception. Supervisors are reluctant to reprove the nursing aides for fear they will quit and leave them even more shorthanded. A kind of bilateral racial rancor probably also plays a part in the reluctance of charge nurses to confront aides.

As for charge nurses, I only have two categories—those who ask if they can help or at least look directly at you when you stop at their circular barricade, and those who steadfastly ignore your presence. Sally, a retired Army nurse, is my favorite, but she was assigned several months ago to Fair Acres's new secured Alzheimer's wing. So now I hope to find Joan on duty when I arrive in the afternoon. She lacks the assertiveness a good supervisor needs, but she maintains a gentle persistence that eventually gets problems taken care of.

When I'm truly desperate, however, I go to Billie, the nursing home's bookkeeper/director's secretary/general receptionist. Billie is one of those people so good that you meet no more than a handful like her in a lifetime. Her desk is always layered with stacks of reports, accounts, and letters. Yet she always finds whatever document I need within minutes. "Sit down," she says immediately, gesturing to one of the visitor-chairs facing her desk. "How can I help you?"

Having the desk between us never seems like a barricade, perhaps because truly awful little knickknacks of the sort you find at craft sales and church bazaars sit atop the computer monitor and among the piles of paper. For a while, Billie even had a wire cage sitting on the floor beside her desk. It held an orphaned baby rabbit her son had found. She fed it with a dropper every hour. Now it lives, full grown, in a corner of the parlor.

Despite being wickedly overworked at Fair Acres, Billie also works a shift at Wal-Mart. This, she tells me, is necessary to keep two of her children in college.

Billie printed out and faxed a total of six times my mother's records to Blue Cross/Blue Shield so that my father could collect for the sixty days of long-term care her policy covers. She made phone calls, both to the insurance company and to the corporation that owns Fair Acres. Never once did she grouse, fret, or stew about doing this. "Just let me know if you need anything else," she always says as I, who often groused, fretted, and stewed during the year it took to retrieve the money, go out the door.

Billie is what my husband calls "a big strapping girl," and her clothes look like what you might see at a fifties-era Pentecostal church. Her glossy brown bangs brush the tops of her oversized eyeglasses. Maybe it's the cinnamon-colored freckles scattered over her nose and cheekbones or the way her eyes widen when she removes her glasses and lets them dangle against her chest, but Billie still looks as if she's twenty years old, sometimes just ten.

When a problem proves absolutely intractable after I've exhausted the normal channels, I go to Billie. A year ago my mother's clothes were disappearing at an alarming rate into the great maw of the institutional laundry. When my mother was first admitted to Fair Acres, my father decided he would wash her clothes himself at home. The administration posted a sign on my mother's closet door: "Resident's laundry is done by her family." But on her three weekly trips to the shower room where my mother is stripped, shampooed, and showered, the bath aides often dumped her clothes into the common hamper that goes to the laundry room on-site.

The Laundry Mafia, identifiable by their pink uniforms and with whom my father waged constant war, refuse to let outsiders, including nurses aides, charge nurses, and, most especially, residents' relatives, into their authorized precincts. When my father cornered them to ask about my mother's clothes, they proved at first indifferent and then defensive.

So I enlisted Billie. But even she failed to gain access to the room housing the stainless steel industrial washers and dryers. I trailed behind her as she went from one department to another—nursing, housekeeping, maintenance. I heard her muttering to herself, "This isn't right. This just isn't right." For those words of vindication, more valuable than the six thousand dollars from the insurance company, I could have fallen at her feet and kissed them.

For the most part, the staff at Fair Acres adopts a defensive posture whenever they see a patient's relative coming. And I can't say I blame them. They work in an atmosphere of constant anger. It thrums from the wheelchairs circling the nurses' station. It ricochets within the residents' families. It radiates from reprimanded aides. No wonder the people behind the circular barricade stare mutely into the middle distance as you deliver your latest complaint.

What a difficult dance we all do up and down those halls. What anguish those walls contain. Old, sick people who feel afraid, abandoned, outraged at what they have become and where they have landed. Husbands, wives, grown children whose hearts are raw with guilt and impotence. Administrators juggling budgets, sweating out Medicaid payments, trolling for employees, and fending off nightmares about lawsuits. Nurses trying to keep their patients' papery thin skin intact, their compacted bowels emptied, and doctors' orders deciphered. Aides working sixteen hours a day, wiping feces from flaccid flanks, lifting fragile bodies bent like wrecked bicycle frames. And then going home to their own families whose needs their salary cannot cover.

Huntsville, my hometown, is most widely known as the place where the state of Texas executes more people than anywhere else in the nation. A journalist from a slick magazine, in town to cover a high-profile execution, recently called to ask if he could interview me since David and I had written a book on the subject. We met for lunch before my afternoon trek to Fair Acres.

"One thing that really surprises me about this place," he said, "is the . . . well, forthright way people talk about executions. I mean they call the place where it happens 'the Death House.'" He gave a little shrug and shook his head. "I guess you've got to give them credit for not trying to sugarcoat it."

Only later, as I pulled into the parking lot at Fair Acres, did it strike me. This low sprawling building is also the Death House. The people who live here are under a death sentence, and their last day is coming, on average, at a faster clip than that of the state's condemned murderers. Some residents here will appeal their case to the local hospital. The IV drips they will receive won't be intended to kill them but to keep their organs functioning for a little while longer. But for them, too, all appeals will eventually run out.

I sat there a moment after I turned off the engine, the key still in my hand. The shift was changing and a woman in a purple uniform was standing in the shade of the portico, smoking a last cigarette. I slipped the car key into my pocket and opened the door. Coming here is hard work for us all. The woman waiting to go on duty, the other regular visitors I would see today, and, most of all, the people who live here. We all breathe in anger and anguish with the air. Which is why the hardest work of all, yet the only thing that keeps us human, is behaving with whatever kindness we can muster for one another.

9

Guilt and the Severed Self

In *The Once and Future King*, T. H. White's retelling of the legend of King Arthur, Merlin admonishes the young prince that every time you tell a lie, you kill a piece of the world. Long before my mother went to Fair Acres, my world had developed a major case of gangrene when my mother started lying about her medications.

Sometimes she would move the little plastic amber tubes to a different cabinet and then claim not to know where her pills were. Or she would hide a new prescription the doctor had just written in the side pocket of her purse. When I uncovered these pitiful attempts at concealment, she would claim to have no idea how the pills or prescriptions came to be there.

Strictly speaking, of course, she wasn't really lying. Any psychiatrist or moral theologian would be careful to distinguish between the actions of people in control of their faculties and behavior affected by illness. I knew this. At least my head knew it. And even large portions of my heart. But the first time you realize your mother has told you a lie, something inside on the cellular level rebels, rises up, and howls "No!"

Living daily on that border between reason and delusion

sapped my own sanity. What's wrong with me? I kept asking myself. Why can't I get a grip here? What I wanted to say, wanted to be able to say, was: Okay, I can handle this. I *should* handle this. It's not that complicated. After all, I only spend a few hours a day with my mother.

So why couldn't I even manage a trip to Wal-Mart? Why couldn't I sleep?

One night I lay in bed, staring up at the ceiling. I hadn't had a decent night's sleep in weeks. I recalled with some bitterness the psalm that advises us to remember the Lord upon our bed and to meditate on him "in the night watches." It wasn't exactly the Lord I was meditating on these sleepless nights, but my own anguish.

I switched on the bedside lamp and riffled through my *Book of Common Prayer*. Psalm 16. "I will bless the Lord who gives me counsel; my heart teaches me, night after night." I closed the book, turned off the light, and flopped back on my pillow.

"Okay," I said into the darkness. "Let's have some counsel. And this better be good."

But the tape loop in my brain started over again. What's wrong with me? Is there something I'm denying here? That my mother has a horrible and incurable disease? That she will die? I don't think so. So why can't I get a grip?

But maybe trying to get a grip was itself the problem. The suggestion formed silently in my consciousness. Maybe there's no grip to be gotten. Doctors often say about a patient in extremis, "Her systems have begun to fail, to shut down." And, the darkness went on whispering mercilessly, every system eventually fails. Including you.

I don't like that word, failure. But it seemed, finally, the right one. Whatever word my mother was struggling with in her own dark night, mine was "failure."

As they begin their downward journey into the Inferno, the Roman poet Virgil advises Dante that, in order to survive this ordeal without losing his own intellect or, indeed, his soul, he must "put by all division of spirit and gather your soul against all cowardice."

Good advice. But how, I wanted to know, was I to keep my spirit undivided while I watched my mother's own descent into hell? By what means does one gather one's soul against cowardice? Prayer? Prozac? Triage training?

You hear stories of firefighters entering burning buildings to retrieve people trapped inside, and you secretly wonder if you would have that kind of courage. Or you read about a bystander who plunges into a raging river to rescue a drowning child, and you calculate your own odds of pulling off something like that. I try to imagine myself in the heat and drama of such a moment, having the nerve or guts or heart—whatever soft tissue such hard acts spring from—to behave heroically. I gave myself at least a slim chance of acting courageously in such a brief dramatic moment.

But in the slow unwinding of days, when there was little drama and lots of time to consider, to deliberate, to weigh the cost—what then?

Dante made the entire transit through hell and purgatory to the celestial spheres in three days, Good Friday to Easter. My mother's hell lasted seven years.

During the fifth year, my sister-in-law's father was dying in New Orleans, doubtless of lung cancer. Months before, the doctor had discovered a suspicious shadow on his chest x-ray and said it looked like a tumor, but Susan's father opted not to have any tests to confirm the diagnosis. His lungs were already too fragile to risk whittling on anyway. The coughing and wheezing were bad enough, he said. What was the point of adding to his misery with chemotherapy? So he went home to ride it out in his recliner.

He is—or was—a big man, a hard drinker, a heavy smoker, a tough father, and a genetic Roman Catholic.

"He's such a poot," Susan tells me, starting to cry, "and I love him so much."

She'd just returned from a trip home to see him. She is stunned by how fast he's declining. "He looks like an AIDS patient. Skin and bones." She starts to cry again. "I'm sorry," she says. "I was there for six days and bawled the whole time. Now I'm home and I'm still crying."

Her older sister, being temporarily unattached, had moved back home when their father fell in the laundry room and their mother couldn't budge him.

"He won't sleep in the bed, so my sister makes up the couch fresh everyday. He's got a potty chair like your mother's right beside it. He can lift himself onto it most of the time. But he also insists on a waste basket so he can just piss off the side when it's too much trouble to move." She makes a sound between a snort and a laugh. "It's just a constant thing—do you want this, do you want that?—trying to please him." She draws a shaky breath.

"I know," I say. "You're desperate to do something to make it better. And naturally he's fretful, being so sick and miserable."

"I couldn't believe it was the same man." She blows her nose and tries to laugh. "And my mother—the Queen of Denial."

"You don't mean she can't see that—"

"No! It's unbelievable. She keeps saying things like, 'He could get up and go on, walk, if he just wanted to.' My sister gives him morphine, just at night so far. She takes away his cigarettes then."

"So he's still smoking?" I blurt, then quickly add, "But why not, I guess. I mean, at this point."

"At least he finally agreed to hospice. On a limited basis anyway. He was falling so often I think he got scared. My sister's strong. She lifts weights, but there's a limit to her strength. And she's going to have to leave soon. She's about done in."

"What will they do then?"

"A facility, I guess. Mom can't handle it. I'm going back in a couple of weeks. We're all supposed to converge there. A family powwow."

"Should be interesting," I say. Susan's siblings run the gamut from lawyer to drug addict.

She groans. "I think it's easier—I mean I know it's hard for you there with your mother—but when you see them every day, it's not such a shock. You get used to it a little at a time."

"You're probably right," I say, even though I'm not sure this is true.

I thought about those first weeks after I came home, remembering how undone I was. No way is easier, I think, but some are shorter. Cancer will have its way with Susan's father soon now. A couple more months at most and it will be over.

I sometimes wonder, if I had known, not how hard it would be, but how long my mother's dwindling would last, whether I would have had the courage to take on the job. Fortunately, I acted—on impulse, and not for the first time, with life-changing consequences. But what if I had been able to see into the future, to tote up the bill ahead of time? Would I have had the courage to choose this course then?

This is when it doesn't pay to have an imagination, to be able to picture yourself in different situations. Because I can see myself, holding the cash register tape and gasping in horror at the bottom line. And for even that imagined, hypothetical hesitation, I feel guilty.

I can conceive of countless ways by which, on any given day, I could have done better at this job, could have discovered some play therapy or language adaptation technique that would have helped my mother to communicate better. Offered some stimulation to her remaining senses that would, if not restore or salvage her damaged faculties, at least have entertained her. The foam football I brought for games of catch in her room at Fair Acres lay in the chest of drawers, another failure. She didn't touch, after a few months, the sketch pad and colored markers with which she once labored to fill in the corners of stenciled figures. Surely I could have been more inventive than that.

Our daily routine came down to this: After sending my father off to take his afternoon nap, I would turn my mother onto her right side using the technique the aides had taught me, so that she could rest her cracked pelvis. Sometimes I would lie down beside her then, my head at the foot of her bed, my feet on the window sill; this made her feel secure enough to sleep a while. Or, if she was too tired to want even that reassurance, I would sit in her wheelchair and scan the headlines of the local paper. After she'd slept about an hour I would wake her for a mid-afternoon snack of cranberry juice and cheese-flavored Pringles, along with any treat I'd brought that day—cherries or watermelon chunks or chocolate. After that came getting her onto and off the potty chair for her daily bowel movement, an operation that requires one or two of the aides. Finally, we watched *Great Chefs of the World* or *Reading Rainbow* on TV. Cooking is an activity she still recognized, and she liked seeing the children who do the book reviews on PBS. That was as inventive as I got after the first year.

Why badger her with schemes to make her better? That was how I justified my own exhausted spirit and depleted imagination.

What never goes away, doesn't wear out or disappear, is the feeling—no, the certain knowledge—that I could have done more, done better.

On the left side of the nave at my church, right up on the front pew close to the organ, sits my friend Jody. She's there every Sunday except in late summer when she's working at the Houston Renaissance Festival. Jody is an actress and, among other gigs, plays the part of Hearty Nan the Hostess, dressed up in sixteenth-century velvet décolletage. At church, her son sits beside her, whenever he's not serving as acolyte. On her other side, her father, Hank, perches on the edge of the pew, bolt upright.

Hank lives in the garage Jody and her husband converted into an apartment for him several years ago when his Alzheimer's got too bad for him to live alone any longer.

Jody is short, maybe five-two at most, and Hank isn't any taller. He usually wears an ice-cream suit, his black-rimmed glasses slipping halfway down his nose and his white pompadour combed smartly back. When he walks, he takes small steps, constantly scanning from side to side in quick, jerky motions, which makes him look like a bantam rooster. His manner is slightly combative; at times he's been "suspended" for scuffling at the Senior Center where he goes in the mornings.

I've talked to Hank in that patronizing way we "reach out" to such people. "How are you this morning, Hank?" I ask, my voice Sunday school bright.

"Can I smoke in here?" he barks, taking a pipe from his pocket.

During the service, Hank sometimes swivels sideways in the pew, following the progress of the ushers down the aisle with the collection plates. He fidgets nervously when Jody gets up to join the choir during the anthem. If the rector makes a joke, Hank swings around, scanning the congregation, trying to catch what everyone is laughing about. At communion he advances to the rail with his small, quick steps and takes the wafer from the priest with a fierce grimace.

On the same side of the nave, several rows back, sit Miranda, and her mother, Violet. Miranda has astonishingly dark glossy hair, cut short, and thick, dramatic eyelashes. Miranda's son is there, too, at least his physical remains. His ashes occupy one of the small brass cubicles in the columbarium at the rear of the nave where a number of our cremated members rest.

Violet, one can see, was once a beauty, and, indeed, even at her present age—I'd guess around seventy—she retains her willowy figure. Her gray hair is always swept up in a wispy French twist. Her genteel voile dresses are sprinkled with pastel flowers. But sometimes her facial features slip uncertainly off center. She clutches a handkerchief in one hand. Her eyes flutter nervously to her daughter's face, as though checking for the appropriate expression or the cue to stand or kneel.

Violet, like Hank, has Alzheimer's. Like Hank, she lives with her daughter. One day Hank and Violet, like my mother, will probably go to a nursing home. My mother, on the other hand, never did live in her daughter's home—my home. The one thing that might have made her happy.

I tell myself there were several good reasons for this, the chief one being my father. He would have been devastated if she had chosen to live with me rather than in their home, a scant half-mile down the road. How could I have taken her from him? Caring for her during her long illness has been his salvation in more ways than one.

What if I had contrived to move them both into my house? My mother would not have liked that arrangement. And did I have the right to make that kind of choice for them? To embroil us all in a potential battle of wills?

Yet, however I try to mitigate the answers to these questions, I know I could never have handled my mother's fears, her night-time rambles looking for intruders, her hallucinations and constant need, twenty-four hours a day. Not for long anyway.

This is why I cringe when anyone congratulates me on having been "such a good daughter." I know how relative "good" is.

In the olden days, when Sears still sent out fat catalogues full of household goods and appliances, they labeled a number of their products "good," "better," and "best." That's how I measure what it means to be a good daughter. Jody and Miranda are better, maybe even best.

I don't like being praised for "caregiving." Frankly, I don't even like the word. It's one of those linguistic inventions by well-meaning people, intended, I suppose, to emphasize the generosity, the magnanimity of the one doing the job. "Care-taking," the term it supplanted, must have somehow implied drudgery or coercion. But the job does *take* care. You wrest the caring from wherever within you it resides. That spot more often feels like the horny soles of your feet than the softer tissue of the heart. You do what you do however you can. And it's always little enough.

I'm not trolling for reassurance or consolation here. Please don't tell me that we all have to learn what our limits are. I'm all too familiar with mine. And I've given myself a good, solid C. I've done an acceptable job. To claim more than that, despite my friends' urgings, would not fit what I feel on the inside. To collude in disguising one's interior reality when presenting the self to the outside world is how you end up with a divided spirit, the danger against which Virgil cautioned Dante. The surest way of dividing the spirit, I have found, is to speak with a double tongue.

10
Losing Language

Mental, cognitive, intellect—are these all different categories? Does one fit within another like nested dolls? How do they connect to one's physical being, to nerves, synapses, motor skills? What binds brain to body? Mind to brain? Soul to self?

These are the questions that consumed me as I watched this woman who once memorized medical vocabularies, who quoted reams of Scripture, who juggled employee rosters and payrolls, as she dissolved into a puddle of unknowing.

I had already discovered that my mother's brain was not producing dopamine properly. Without this neurotransmitter, the electrical impulses, which ordinarily would signal her muscles to move, get jammed or misdirected. This accounted for her slowed and uncertain gait, laggard speech, hand tremors. All classic Parkinson's symptoms.

I knew too that the substantia nigra, the bit of brain tissue responsible for producing dopamine, dies more rapidly in Parkinson's patients than in the rest of us. The drug levadopa, popularly known as L-dopa, has until recently been the only medication available for treating the disease. Once absorbed by the brain, L-dopa is converted to dopamine.

One might conclude, as I did, that treating Parkinson's was thus a simple matter of adding the right amount of L-dopa at the right time. Like mixing gasoline and oxygen in the proper ratio so spark plugs can fire the car engine. But here I fell victim to an inadequate paradigm. For one thing, a car engine, even at its peak performance, never produces its own gasoline. An automobile's internal organs do not whisper messages to one another along extended pathways. Not even the computerized sensors in newer models come close to approximating the delicate interchanges that transpire between biochemicals in the body.

Synthetic L-dopa is no mere gas tank additive. For one thing (I would not learn this for another year), once you have started adding L-dopa to your brain, you can never stop taking the drug. Put a healthy person with no previous Parkinson symptoms on L-dopa and, should he stop taking the medication, he will develop tremor and other manifestations of the disease. Like a malingerer on the dole, the dopamine-producing section of the brain quits working if it knows it can depend on chemical welfare.

Also, L-dopa, while the most effective treatment for Parkinsonian symptoms, is also the most problematic. My mother struggled with the overwhelming waves of nausea it caused, even though the form she took also contained carbidopa, an additive designed to reduce L-dopa's side effects.

Hallucinations, I learned, were yet another unwelcome consequence of the drug. I remembered references to hallucinations in some of the Parkinson's books my mother had read so avidly the first summer. Most of these were casual allusions to visual distortions, made almost airily, as though they were a minor inconvenience. Firsthand accounts by patients who hallucinated on the drug treated their visions as a joke. One woman reported setting an extra place at the table for the "guest"—invisible to everyone else but her.

To my mother, however, hallucinations had been no joke. She connected the term to drugs like marijuana and LSD. Making any allusion to her hallucinations would have been tantamount to accusing her of drug addiction.

It is easy to get caught in the vortex of dementia. How do you tell if a person is describing a real or an imagined incident? How do you quantify the content of their conversation? Can you believe 90 percent of what they say? Less? Half? And how do you filter the fiction from the facts?

Did she really misplace the prescription slip or is this merely a ruse to keep you from filling it? Did she really receive a phone call from your brother? The doctor's office?

While she had still been at home, I had guessed wrong in such situations. Doubt poisoned the atmosphere, pumped up the paranoia. You hate being suspicious; she hates being accused. You contrive unobtrusive ways to check facts. She, in turn, becomes defensive and isolated.

We are sitting at her dining table, eating lunch, my father and mother, our cousin Margaret, and me. Margaret is trying to entertain us with tales of her new litter of barn cats.

"They get up under the house—I can't for the life of me figure out where they're getting in. Half a dozen of them."

"That many?" I say.

"Yes. They get to chasing and carrying on. It makes a terrible racket."

"I can believe it," my father puts in, shaking his head.

My mother looks up sharply, then back at her plate. "I wish someone would do that for me."

"Do what?" I ask.

"Believe what I say."

What, I was still wondering at the end of that first year, should be my response to the obvious fabrications of her imagination? Should I contradict her? Expose the fantasies for what they were? Should I just ignore them? Play along? What, after all, do you say to someone who tells you, quite seriously, that people are building Buddhist temples in the pines behind her house? If I challenged this account or even gently explained the outlandishness of such a claim, she first got angry and then remote.

My father took the path of least resistance, accommodating her fears of invasion by propping chairs under all the doorknobs before they went to bed at night. But his accommodation did not lessen my mother's panic and dread. She continued to get him up in the middle of the night to search for intruders, then grew angry when he failed to find any.

Exasperated, I took the opposite tack, steadfastly denying all her delusions.

"No, Mother," I would say when she insisted the puddle I drove through was blood or seeping oil. "It's just water. Remember? It rained last night."

Doggedly I pointed out logical inconsistencies.

"See?" I would say as we took our afternoon walk down the lane. "There's been no fire here. Do you see any ashes, any burn marks on the trees?" But my reasoning only made her keep these realities to herself.

I could see that my strategy was no more successful than my father's.

I searched the library, the Internet, disease newsletters for advice. Nothing. I called my cousin, the psychologist. "So what do I do?" I wailed. "If I play along, pretend there really are Buddhist temples down in the woods—my brother, by the way, is supposedly in on this conspiracy—if I show concern about Indians attacking the house, won't that undermine whatever grasp she still has on reality?"

"Beats me," my cousin said. "I've never really had to deal with this problem. That's not my population. People in that shape generally end up in institutions."

Once, as I sat on the bed beside my mother, holding her hand, she wept from frustration because I wouldn't admit there were strangers in the attic.

"No one believes me," she cried.

"I believe you, Mother," I heard myself saying. "It is real—real to you." And for a time I was proud of this answer. It offered affirmation if not agreement. But it neither fooled nor satisfied her. She saw through my subterfuge.

Physical disabilities I could handle. And I would have laughed at the loss of mental infirmities of the merely cognitive sort—

the spelling and math. Memory loss I could understand, compensate for. But her dark imaginings threatened to undo me because they undid her. They expunged the woman I knew as my mother. Defaced all that I admired and honored in her.

Like most people living close to a life-altering disease, I checked myself constantly, convinced from time to time that I too had Parkinson's, even though I knew it is neither contagious nor, generally speaking, hereditary.

Learning how rudimentary medical knowledge of the disease is, I was skeptical even of that reassurance. Initially, if a cup shook in my hand, if I missed a step going up the stairs, I took it as the first sign that my brain was starved for dopamine.

Though I learned in time to discount these fears, what did not go away was the old vertiginous uncertainty about selfhood. If my mother, as we say, was not herself, then who was she? What was she? What, come to that, were any of us?

How—by what process—do you become another self? Or perhaps no one at all? It is easy for anyone who has lived with dementia to consider demon possession a real possibility. Those Bible stories of people infested with evil spirits made perfect sense to me. They go as far as most other verbal formulations to explain what's going on; they are the anti-self, the not-oneself overwhelming the true self. The demon theory pictures the self locked up and brutalized by marauding invaders. The medical explanation posits a self stupefied by chemical starvation. But whether we say "dementia" or "demons," both terms assume that some entity called the self actually exists, that it is not simply some fancy we have invented.

Some of the worst damage to my mother's brain showed up as aphasia, a loss in the ability to speak or to comprehend written or spoken language. This became more severe as the months went by. Aphasia put up enormous obstacles to our life together. I was often uncertain that she understood what I said to her. She would sometimes frown and ask me to repeat; my words either hadn't registered or hadn't been recognized. Sometimes she merely turned away, as if the effort to understand was too great or the results too disheartening.

Communication between my parents, never too good at the best of times, was even more difficult. My mother's voice was weak and my father's hearing poor. Many people tended to talk over her, asking a question and then not giving her enough time to respond before they rattled on, either impatient or uncomfortable with more than a few seconds of silence.

I found little scraps of paper on the bureau or nightstand in her room with letters or numbers written on them in her, by then, tiny, quavering script. None of them made any sense.

My father came across a letter to Ann Landers in the paper one day about an Alzheimer's patient who was helped by reading aloud, so he began bringing her the local newspaper to read every morning. But though my mother made out a few words, she couldn't understand what they meant.

Her own speech fluctuated widely. On good days she could form short sentences, and, if we were talking about something right before us—her glass of cranberry juice or her wheelchair—the sentences sometimes even made sense. "The phone is ringing," or "I don't want that." Often though, she had to grope for an accurate word and only hit one near it in sound or meaning. "Turn off the balloon," she might say, and I'd know, somehow, that she meant the air-conditioner.

"What did you have for lunch?" I would ask.

"A few steamed scrimmage," she replied. "Or something that looked like shammy."

Sometimes she realized the word she'd used wasn't the one she intended, more often not. In the midst of searching for the word she meant, she would sometimes try to spell it. But the letters—never more than three—were random. "P, T, N," she might say, frowning with the effort to bring forth language.

Her pronouns never had clear referents, probably because names eluded her. "Where do they live now?" she would ask me suddenly.

"Who, Mother?"

"You know," she insisted, obviously believing I was only pretending ignorance. "The people who moved."

"Moved?" And I would give my usual answer to these murky inquiries.

"I'm not sure."

She understood all time as now, all space as here. Her mental difficulties were not quite the same as the Alzheimer's type of memory-loss. In fact, her memory—when she could find the language to verbalize it—was not bad. Her sense of time and space, like that of a young child, was dominated by the present. She could not juggle temporal or spatial abstractions any better than a three-year-old who asks "are we there yet?" from the back seat of the car.

Trying to overcome her depleted conversation skills, she would sometimes employ metaphors whose referents were known only to her. When she had a bowel movement, for instance, she was "making little houses."

Sometimes I would laugh and make a joke of her strange locutions, and she would laugh too. Those were the good days.

On most days, however, she merely rambled, beginning lengthy narratives of some fantasy trip or encounter with distant family members which would proceed for a phrase or two in one direction, then make sudden oblique turns into blind alleys. The words meandered like a trickle of water across packed dry dirt, its sporadic progress gradually drying up. At such times she seemed unaware of her aphasia, evidently taking pleasure in the simple process of speech. She could keep talking for half an hour at a stretch, never suspecting that her tales were disjointed and impenetrable. All the characters were pronouns or, at most, generic—"that boy," "those people." If I was able to catch her general drift, I tried to play along, ask her questions, just to keep her talking.

"Here," she'd say, pushing toward me a blanket she'd wadded into a ball, "take this to her and tell them it's all I could get done."

"Okay, Mother. I'm sure they'll understand. This is all they'll need anyway."

On bad days, neither I nor anyone else could make even meager sense of what she tried to mean. The sounds were no longer sentences or even words, just garbled syllables. "At night . . . take shy . . . wargen . . . sima, sima." These unsuccessful struggles with words used to embarrass me. When she came out with a long string of incomprehensible syllables and looked at me insistently, urgently, expecting me to respond, I could only stare at her. How do you tell someone, in a nice way, that they're babbling? At some point, even pretense is impossible.

When I was no longer able to follow a thread of meaning, I had to admit I was lost. "I'm sorry, Mother. I can't understand. The words aren't coming out right." Sometimes she tried again, even more urgently, but never with any better success. Other times, she simply sighed and closed her eyes and gave up. I was not sure which was worse. I mopped tears from the well of her eye socket during a conversation in which the only word of hers I understood was "lonely."

There was another kind of day, too, whose category was ambiguous. It was bad in that she scarcely recognized where she was. Her words became mere cooings, half-whispered, half-sung syllables. Yet she didn't seem upset. In fact, she could have a remarkably gentle spirit, even smile contentedly. I suspect she might not have even recognized me then. *There*, I think, *she's gone. Over the edge. Beyond the pale. To never-never land.*

On those days her fear seemed to have disappeared. And I found I preferred this state. In fact, I felt a remarkable sense of lightness, of relief. Taking care of this dazed creature lying in the bed was almost like tending a baby. Irritation, anxiety disappeared for me too. Tenderness returned.

This relief, however, was short-lived. She always came back.

"If she would just go away and stay away," I told Margaret. "I could live with that. But this coming and going—here one day and gone the next—it's like burying Lazarus over and over again."

11

Which Brain?

Almost every day for months after the move to the nursing home my mother would ask me where she would sleep that night.

"Why here, of course," I would tell her. "This is your room."

"No," she protested. "She told me I had to get out of here. I'm kicked out." There was no use asking who "she" was; my mother can never give pronouns referents. "She" was simply archetypal Authority.

Some days she would say, "I saw your sister Joyce today."

"Oh?" I no longer bothered to point out that Joyce is her sister, not mine.

"But she was in a hurry. She pretended she didn't see me."

Sometimes it was my brother she'd spotted in the hall but who ignored her. Or, more rarely, a friend. And these sentences, though halting, were often remarkably coherent for someone with aphasia as severe as my mother's.

Often, around the noon hour, my mother would have panic attacks. Her breathing would grow rapid and shallow. Her heart raced. She panted for breath. She would stare at me wildly.

Breathe slow, I would whisper to her, breathe slower, the only thing I could think of to say.

Over the next months the three of us, my father, my mother, and I, settled into our nursing home routine. The very routine itself appeared to have a calming effect on my mother's fears. Her physical and mental states continued to decline, however.

About six months after my mother entered Fair Acres, I made an outline of what I judged to be her current mental state. Her problems, I believed, could be divided into the categories of Memory, Reasoning, Aberrations/Deficits, and Emotions.

Her dementia was not then the typical Alzheimer's type, though several of her symptoms were similar. Usually Alzheimer's disease first shows itself in loss of short-term memory, but this was not a problem for my mother at that point. She could usually recall, though she might not be able to say their names, the people who had visited her recently.

She also retained some sense of impending events, though, like a young child, she couldn't judge the length of time until they would happen. To my mother, anything in the future was imminent. The ability to use abstractions for time and space was gone. Consequently, her short-term memory worked only for concrete events.

For example, she didn't know what day it was, ever. Time for her, as Isaac Watts's hymn puts it, is "an everflowing stream," indivisible and whole, rather than an accumulation of distinct moments.

Also, her ability to recollect details in sequence was out the window. And, most frustrating to me, she could not recall that she could neither walk nor stand.

As for her long-term memory, she remembered most of the family, and, much of the time, whether they were living or dead. Friends were another matter, however. Memories of her more distant past were either lost to her or she was unwilling to talk about them. Unlike my grandfather, who retold stories of World War I or boyhood hunting adventures, my mother never

talked about her childhood or recalled earlier times with her
brothers and sisters.

As for reasoning, only the simplest and most immediate
cause-and-effect relationships made sense to her, and even those
had to be connected to some motor skill. She understood, for
instance, that if you turn loose of a glass, it will fall to the floor.
Beyond that, sequence and causation were lost on her. This
meant she could not understand why she was in a nursing home
or why I had to leave her.

Under the category of Aberrations/Deficits in my outline, I
listed hallucinations and fantasizing, examples of which I've
described earlier. Strangely enough, her hallucinations did not
seem as frightening once she moved to the nursing home.
When she "saw" people now, they were usually one of her sisters or my brother, not the shadowy figures that had once
threatened to come in through her bedroom window at home.

Her sheets and blankets often became some kind of sewing
or handwork. She imagined she had gone to the grocery store
or church or a meeting. But never, I noticed, that she had visited other family members.

Perhaps strangest of all, however, was her inability to separate dreams from waking. One state was as real to her as the
other; she made no distinction between them. Her belief in the
reality of dreamed events remained unshakeable. In fact, many
of her fantasy narratives may actually have been dreams she was
recounting.

I try to imagine what that would be like—believing that the
dream I had last night really happened. A world as wild and
fluid as that, full of shifting scenes and morphing characters,
would terrify me. Who, after all, could remain sane in a world
as unstable as that?

Under Aberration/Deficit, I also listed my mother's aphasia,
her difficulties with language, along with certain physical manifestations that might be labeled an "obsessive-compulsive" disorder.

Her hands are constantly busy—folding, patting, smoothing, picking. Her fingertips rub together as if testing the texture

of some invisible fabric. Even in her sleep her hands move, the long fingers shuffling the objects of her dreaming.

I pondered a good while before labeling the final category Emotions. We tend to consider feeling and thinking opposing categories. In fact, as a culture we've invested a good bit in that notion. Somehow it's easier for us to accept that our cognitive functions can be damaged by trauma or disease than that our very love or hate, our joy and sorrow, hang by so physical, and thus so flimsy, a thread. You can lose your ability to speak or think straight and not have lost all. You're still a human being. But if your feelings blow a fuse, if the wires to desire or despise get crossed, then the self suddenly becomes unrecognizable.

When we react strangely to a situation, our friends may say, That's not like her. Sometimes we may even fail to recognize ourselves.

We've gotten used to the idea that our rationality can be tinkered with. We've learned that our perceptions can be fooled, our judgment befuddled by alcohol, drugs, and lack of sleep. But knowing that our emotions are at the mercy of our body's chemistry makes us profoundly uneasy. Our feelings are more truly us somehow, closer to the center of the self. The notion that our emotions, as well as our thinking, are a mere function of the physical brain unnerves us. People who willingly take antibiotics for an infection or ginkgo biloba to boost their memory can balk at accepting a prescription for antidepressants or bipolar disorder. They have a dread, not of losing their mind, but of forfeiting their very selves.

I coped with the knotty problem of my mother's emotions in my usual way. I went to the library, checked out Sherwin Nuland's *The Wisdom of the Body,* and studied the section on the brain. The cerebrum, that convoluted, slightly flattened ball, is what one ordinarily sees in illustrations of the brain. If you cut a hole in the top of the skull, you could see those wrinkled corrugations shining slick and gray. These are the famous "little gray cells" on which Agatha Christie's detective, Hercule Poirot, relies in order to solve mysteries.

But this gray matter, the cerebral cortex, is less than a quarter-inch thick, about the depth of a grapefruit rind. True enough, it performs the act we call thinking. But beneath it lies a massive network of white fibers, the brain's communication system, which makes up the bulk of the brain. In order to think, evaluate, weigh, ponder, analyze, or reason, the gray matter must have the information that wiring network carries.

Lower than the white matter, at the back of the head atop a shelf formed by the skull's inward curve, sits a fibrous knot known as the cerebellum. This brain chunk coordinates the movement of the voluntary muscles, making it possible for one to walk, kick a ball, chop onions, raise an eyebrow.

Those two main structures, the cerebrum and the cerebellum, are the only parts of the brain visible when you cut away the bony skull. Everything else, the components that govern your involuntary actions, the kind that can't wait for reason—breathing, heartbeat, hormones—are submerged beneath the cerebrum's soft mass.

When the spinal cord rises from its casing of vertebrae and emerges in the head, it becomes the brainstem or medulla. In this crucial area, Dr. M, the neurologist, has told me, my mother's leaky or collapsed blood vessels have already caused a great deal of damage. Small pipeline bursts here and there have erased her sense of balance, making it impossible for her to walk or to sit up without pillows wedged in her wheelchair to keep her from toppling over.

Atop the medulla sits the mysterious midbrain, containing the several separate structures of the limbic system. Limbic—as in limbo. To the Romans the word meant hem or fringe. Dante used it to name the antechamber of hell. Virtuous pagans live out eternity there, caught between the two worlds of the tormented and the blessed. In the brain, the limbic system governs that shady region between our inner worlds of reason and emotion.

The brain's limbo harbors the hypothalamus, a tiny organ no larger than a pearl. From this pearl flow all one's emotions or, more precisely, the commands for glands to crank out the electro-chemicals that produce our internal weather.

At this point in brain research, it appears that our earliest emotion, the one with which infants greet the world, is surprise. The only other feelings evident in newborns are distress and pleasure, the latter sometimes expanding into joy.

For the most part, we don't develop anger until we've been around a good four months, when the sensation of physical constriction becomes increasingly unwelcome. (We are only beginning to understand how essential is this developmental period in our emotional lives. If babies are not held, cuddled, or cooed at, they may not receive enough emotional stimulation to learn the difference between distress and pleasure. Thus they become apathetic and as the clinical term has it, "fail to thrive.")

Because my mother was so often afraid, whether of intruders or abandonment, I wanted to know where her fear came from. What taught her to be afraid? The early loss of her mother? Was anxiety a flaw in her character, one that reason once controlled but could no longer keep at bay? Was it an unpleasant side-effect of her medications? What could I do to reassure her, to relieve those fears?

We think of fear as instinctual, built-in. Yet those who study such matters say we have to live in this world a full six months before we learn to be truly afraid.

Rhesus monkeys raised in captivity display no fear when introduced to animals that, in their normal environment, are their natural enemies. Show them a snake, for instance, and they may be curious but not afraid. Show them a video, however, of another monkey reacting fearfully to a snake, and afterward they too will be terrified when they see a snake, whether a real one or a facsimile.

So, one might conclude, fear is indeed a learned emotion. But it's not as simple as that. The brain and its workings seldom are. We picture its various structures as compartments, rooms with closed doors, behind which the occupants are carrying out their assigned tasks like workers in office cubicles. In this paradigm, the thalamus, a hunk of tissue the size of a large egg located just beneath the cerebellum, acts as the office manager, routing incoming sensory messages from the outside world to the region of the brain responsible for dealing with smell, sight, texture, taste, or sound. The thalamus guards against the tendency of the cerebral cortex, the "thinking" part of the brain, to micromanage the entire system, including most of our life-support functions.

Like any good secretary, the thalamus doesn't allow the upper-brain boss to distract itself with what can be handled by a lower-grade employee. An auspicious arrangement, since it means we don't have to actually think about when to breathe or blink our eyes.

Of course, certain adepts—yogis, for instance—can train themselves to stimulate limbic cells and alter otherwise involuntary bodily functions, like heart rate or temperature. Most of us, however, are glad we don't have to think about breathing— or digesting or even blinking our eyes; otherwise we'd never get to the multiplication tables. The lower parts of the brain function more smoothly without our rational interference.

But as in every office, a good bit of information gets picked up around the water cooler instead of through official channels. So too some incoming messages to the brain don't always get filtered through the thalamus. Researchers have yet to figure out how those work.

Take the case of the Rhesus monkeys raised in sheltered captivity. Show them a video of a monkey reacting fearfully to a flower instead of a snake, and they won't develop a flower phobia.

Why not? What accounts for the difference in the reaction to the snake video and the flower video? Is there a yet deeper stratum of innate knowledge to which they refer?

Ordinarily, the thalamus routes stimuli requiring interpretation to the cerebrum, the upper, reasoning brain. If the cerebrum interprets the stimuli as threatening or dangerous, it then signals instructions to the amygdala, an almond-shaped bit of gray matter buried in the brain's core. The amygdala, which keeps cross-indexed files of memory, instinct, and emotion, in turn releases the appropriate biochemicals, adrenaline for instance, to supercharge the muscles, heart, and lungs, along with the message: run! or, attack!

If the situation proves sufficiently dire, it stores a record of that incident in living color and high-contrast lighting, just to make sure we don't forget it.

With certain stimuli, however, particularly loud or unfamiliar sounds, the thalamus bypasses the upper brain altogether and sends the signal directly to the amygdala. The amygdala then takes matters into its own hands and goes into hyperdrive, dousing the body with a flash flood of hormones and peptides. Thus, that apparently groundless, irrational anxiety or dread one may sometimes experience occurs because the amygdala has galloped off with the entire body in some default-setting direction. In a heartbeat, your body has turned into a toxic chemical dumpsite for no clear reason.

That's only one example, of course, of how the brain can misfire. At any moment, some little scrap of tissue can simply stop doing its job, say producing or regulating certain chemicals. Let the wellspring of serotonin dry up, for instance, and a formerly buoyant person can sink into inexplicable apathy.

I noted in the Emotion part of my outline that my mother, who had been known for her complete command of her emotions, now had little control over them. Her former self-control was never cold or distant—far from it. Her devotion, like God's, endured seemingly forever as numerous friends and family members can attest. Her sympathies had not been deterred by ingratitude. Her anger, like gun powder, had burned hot but dissipated quickly. She had never held grudges. Though occasions for gaiety and laughter had come to her infrequently, she was always eager to welcome them. Sadness and self-pity, on the other hand, she had always worked hard to shake off.

Yet these admirable emotional qualities seem to have sunk into some miry bog, leaving her unprotected from fear and distrust. Most days, I could not get her to smile, much less laugh. Despite her active fantasy life, she found it impossible to imagine herself in someone else's shoes.

Thus her enormous generosity of spirit evaporated. She could not perform the mental operations necessary, for instance, to compare her situation to that of others in the nursing home, some of whom were completely isolated from family and friends. Nor could she any longer call on the soldierly bravery she once advocated for my brother and me.

Nevertheless, as I've said, anger keeps up a steady thrum in nursing homes. I've seen ninety-year-old women sitting in the Fair Acres parlor who would have come to blows if they had been able to reach one another from their wheelchairs. Nursing aides have shown me purple bruises inflicted by an irate, bedridden resident.

Yet anger eluded my mother there, at least in its more overt forms. It was like a muscle she never learned to use and which has atrophied. Instead, she substituted passive aggression for anger. If I left town and didn't see her for several days, she might refuse to speak or even look at me when I returned. Sometimes, having dreamed that we had neglected or abandoned her, she would accuse us the next day with a baleful, silent stare.

But after she had been at Fair Acres several months my mother experienced a single moment of, if not triumph, at least the satisfaction of expressing anger directly. I heard about it from the charge nurse who stopped me when I arrived at Fair Acres one afternoon.

"I don't know what got into your mother this morning," she told me, her eyes round with reconstituted surprise. "She was very upset at breakfast. She even threw her carton of milk across the table. And then she picked up her plate and dumped it on the floor. Poor Mrs. Hawley and Mrs. Novak were simply flabbergasted. That's not like your mother to behave like that." The nurse shook her head. "Not at all like her."

I stood there a moment, trying to visualize this scene. My mother, who, to my knowledge, had never caused a scene in public in the entire course of her life, throwing a two-year-old's tantrum.

"I'll talk to her," I told the nurse, waiting till I turned away to smile to myself.

"Mother," I said as I was brushing her hair later, "what happened at breakfast this morning?"

She jerked her head toward the window as if she hadn't heard me.

"The nurse said you were upset about something," I went on. "And that you, um, threw something?"

She shakes her head now and her pallid cheeks flush. Her fingers pick at the little square of quilt over her lap as she begins a disjointed narrative of where she went the night before. Then suddenly she stops and her eyes fill with tears. "Trouble," she says.

"No," I answer, putting down the hairbrush and sitting down on the bed to face her. I take her hands in mine. "You're not in trouble. Don't worry." I kiss the bony fingers, repeating, "Don't worry."

"They didn't want me. Don't like me." She grips my fingers and starts to cry again.

"Who, Mother? Who didn't want you?"

"Them. You know. Them."

Lilly, one of the more talkative aides, comes in just then to refill my mother's water pitcher with ice for the afternoon. I ask her if there have been any changes recently, any shifts in my mother's routine.

She raises her eyebrows, considering a minute. "Well, you know they just opened that new Alzheimer's wing. It has its own dining room and so they've switched where some people sit at the tables in the regular dining room. That's all I know."

When she leaves, I ask, "Is that what upset you this morning, Mother? Being at a different table?"

"They didn't like me," she replies, with emphasis.

"Everyone likes you, Mother. Sure they did," I say, not at all sure. "What's not to like? But, you know, they may not like it if you throw your milk at them."

I tug at her fingertips, and when I get her to look up at me again, I'm grinning. "It must have been pretty funny though, huh?"

And I hope that, when she looks away now, it's to hide her own smile.

As I leave, I speak to the charge nurse who confirms that my mother was put at a different table that morning.

"That's it, then, isn't it." I say soberly. "Change is upsetting to anyone in my mother's condition, you know. I'm sure it won't happen again."

And, unfortunately, it didn't.

12

Waiting beside the Rubble

On the outline I made of my mother's mental states I had written this note under the heading of Emotions: "In trying to understand her fantasies, especially the recurrent ones, it's best to consider, not their content, but their emotional tone."

Describing my mother's damaged affective state as mere loss of emotional control oversimplifies the matter. She is never, for example, wild with happiness or overwhelmed by relief. It's only the darker emotions—despair, fear, resentment—that carry her away.

This condition struck me as differing from dementia, or even depression, and I made up another name for it. I borrowed the root from pathos, the Greek word for, among other things, emotion, and called it "depathia."

A few decades ago, brain research revealed that certain mental functions are apportioned to one or the other of the cerebral hemispheres. The left hemisphere does the rational analysis, reading and interpreting complex systems of symbols, similar to the way computers operate. And, like computers, one of the left hemisphere's primary virtues is speed.

The right hemisphere, on the other hand, operates at a more leisurely pace. It takes in the world more directly and visually, organizing its information globally, rather than in sequential symbol strings.

The general public took up these notions so enthusiastically that figuring out if one were left- or right-brain dominant became the latest parlor game. Not surprisingly, most people wanted to be put in the latter category, since the right hemisphere was popularly perceived as the seat of emotion and also of "creativity."

The mind's map has since proved to be much more convoluted than that, however. Emotions don't begin in the cerebral cortex, but deeper down, in those small structures of the inner brain. They only pop to the surface for processing, generally in the frontal regions of both hemispheres.

Those tempted to divide feeling and thinking neatly between the right and left hemispheres of the brain may be surprised to learn that it's the right half of the cerebral cortex that primarily handles the negative emotions. Put a random sampling of people in a room, hook them up to monitors measuring the electrical activity in their brains, and have them sit quietly with their eyes closed. Whoever's feeling down that day will show more action in their right brain hemisphere.

So does brain research indeed confirm our cultural assumption that thinking and feeling make up the two main components of our inner life? Certain functions are farmed out to different sections of the brain, it's true, and damage to that area can mean permanent deficit.

Strokes have damaged my mother's ability to access language and to coordinate motions. But no section of the brain, left or right, cortex or limbic, can work on its own, without help from other parts.

To make matters even more complicated, sometimes the parts work in concert, sometimes in opposition. Try thinking about the muscular process while you're descending a staircase—which muscle is contracting or relaxing, where to place your foot, when to shift your weight—and such thinking could cause you to take a tumble. Your feet work a lot better if you let them mind their own business.

Or take stress, that physical response to emotional pressure we currently blame for contributing to, if not causing, every malady from cancer to cold sores. David suspects my mother's Parkinson 's disease broke into bloom under the strain of caring for her cantankerous ninety-year-old father over a decade before her diagnosis.

So does it even make sense to divide ourselves into a thinking self and a feeling self? Are we really divided down that line into opposing halves? Or are the categories themselves a delusion? Do these almost universally accepted classifications impede our accurate understanding of who we are, what a self is?

The notion of a bipolar self has ancient and global precedent. The East symbolizes the division as a black-and-white circle, the line between the yin and yang making a double curve with a dot of the opposite color in each droplet-shaped side. Though the West has no universal visual symbol for the split self, its verbal analogies—at least till recently—have tended to be vertical, a construction inherited from the Greeks. Rationality, the Greeks figured, ought to govern the unruly passions. Later, Freud gave us a tripartite, though still vertical, design of the inner self. He posited a superego that sits atop the self-interested ego to keep it in line with social norms. Beneath the ego lies the submerged, irrational id.

In its peculiar niche between East and West, ancient Hebrew understanding of the self took a different approach to the human activities of thinking and feeling. Though Hebrew has no word for the general category for emotion, there are plenty of good, solid Hebrew words for specific feelings—love, hate, desire, joy, sorrow, even the ennui of Ecclesiastes. When writers needed a verb to describe the act of feeling, they often used the verb for the physical act of moving. For example, Isaiah writes that the king's "heart was moved, and the heart of his people, as the trees of the wood are moved with the wind."

Likewise, Hebrew understanding of thinking was practical rather than abstract. Hebrew has two main verbs for "thinking."

The root for *chashab* means to weave or fabricate, or, more ominously, to plot or contrive. *Ama*, the other verb, means simply "speak." As for the noun "thoughts," the Hebrew writers put particular emphasis on the insuperable distance between our own thoughts and those of God. But the Hebrews never enshrined thought as abstract ratiocination in the fashion of the Greeks. Philosophy as such failed to interest them. When dealing with questions such as why bad things happen to good people, they tended, like Job, to confront God in a forensic manner, putting the question to him as if cross-examining him in a court of law. Nor was thinking pitted against feeling. Indeed, it was their feelings that led them to speak out or weave plots.

Where ancient Hebrew drew a clear verbal line was between the wise and the foolish. Wisdom was a concept they could get behind. The root appears often throughout the Hebrew Scriptures. Yet wisdom entailed more than merely being bright, more than having a reflective nature. Being wise had at least as much to do with righteousness as with intelligence. Wisdom was a skill, learned by active practice. In this, it may share more with Zen discipline than Greek rationality.

Still, how could any of this historical and linguistic analysis help my mother's poor brain, so tunneled with hemorrhagic trauma that it's a wonder anything works at all? And why did I keep trying to figure it out? Why did I sort through these bits of mushy tissue, searching for the seat and citadel of the self? How rational was it on my part to feel relief upon finding out the function of the amygdala, as if my knowing could stave off her panic attacks or quiet her fears?

On good days she still manages to pull herself together for a visitor, at least for a few minutes, and make small talk, calling on a few patterned phrases I have heard her repeat all her life. Things like "so good to see you" and "thank you for coming." And, providing the visitor doesn't stay too long, he or she may go away believing my mother isn't in such bad shape after all, that Esther is still mentally alert.

But beyond such rote expressions, only those of us who had been with her steadily over the last couple of years can make much sense of what she says.

As time went by, I grew increasingly convinced of one thing, at least: she had an underlying signification system, even in the midst of her dementia. Her intelligence was now entirely emotional. One understood it only by attending to metaphor, not logic. What I watched for were gestures. What I listened for were persistent images. These became the icons through which I recognized whatever self remains to her.

Since her face had lost its expressiveness, largely immobilized in what is called the "mask of Parkinson's," I learned to value her rare smiles and to note what triggered them. I also learned to dread the stony glare that signaled the grip of paranoia.

But there were other gestures just as important, movements that no one would remark on who hadn't known her before this disaster came upon us. The delicate, backward sweeping motion of her fingertips as she brushes away imaginary crumbs. The careful pleating of her sheets into some bit of sewing visible only to her. These small gestures of clearing away and making up are the remnants of what she has always done, what she found value in doing. Making the house shine. Preparing for holidays with laden tables, smoothing the bed sheets to welcome guests. Planting flowers, stitching clothes, finishing paintings with rapt attention to detail. Nothing left messy or half-done.

The day before my brother or my daughters arrive for visits, she spends the afternoon cooking in her nursing home bed, propped up on pillows, handing me the finished dishes to store away.

"Is there enough?" she asks me with a worried look. "Are the beds made?" These are her metaphors for love.

The conversations we have, such as they are, work almost entirely by metaphor. Only someone who pays prolonged attention to the references can learn the language and comprehend the message.

She talks about babies frequently. Babies are crying, needing to be fed, to have beds found for them. One day she asked if her youngest sister, now sixty years old, had had her baby yet.

"Did you know your father wants me to have another baby?" she confided one day. "I told him I didn't want to have any more right now." She smiled slightly, as if she were pleased to have been asked anyway.

Almost every week, someone's getting married. There's a wedding to prepare for or else she's just gone to one. And, less frequently but more darkly, she imagines David and I are divorcing. Sometimes she recounts disagreements with coworkers.

"We were supposed to get fourteen done today, but I told her it was impossible."

"Of course," I agree, "that's far too many."

"There's no way," she murmurs, shaking her head. "I don't care what they say." This was the closest she ever came to acknowledging her disabilities.

My mother, I believe, was not just the sum of her capacity either to think or to feel. She is also, and perhaps most enduringly, her history. The memory of that history stored in her brain may have been destroyed or made inaccessible, like an erased or damaged computer file, but her past was still stored in those absorptions, those gestures.

A friend of mine, who teaches education majors how to deal with handicapped pupils, always asks her students at the beginning of the semester which disability each of them would choose if they had to have one. Their answers vary—deafness, blindness, paraplegia. Then she shocks them with her own choice—profound mental retardation. Even Alzheimer's. "If you lose your memory," she explains, "or if you're very retarded, you just don't realize what you're missing. So you don't suffer from its loss."

People with stroke-related dementia often have no awareness of their disabilities either. I stumbled upon that fact by accident. It helped me understand her condition better, but it has not consoled me.

My hunt for facts about my mother's condition, especially her dementia, seems never to end. I sift through articles in medical journals, newspaper stories, firsthand accounts of care-givers. I try to fit their facts to my own observations.

Early on I read about a strategy called validation therapy used especially with Alzheimer's patients. It distinguishes four successive stages of dementia: disorientation, time confusion, repetitive motions, and a final vegetative state. The therapy aims at helping people resolve certain emotional conflicts before they reach that final stage when the cause of their inter-nal discord will no longer be available to their memory.

One would think that forgetting the cause would also elim-inate the resulting pain. However, the emotion, like a melody, lingers on long after its source is forgotten. Anger, fear, regret can wander through the ruins of our brains like ghosts. Or, to return to the musical analogy, like a tune that gets stuck in our heads long after we've forgotten the words. Feelings stick with us a lot longer than the events that prompted them.

The recurrent themes of my mother's fantasies certainly sup-port this view. In the disconnected, dreamlike tales she spun, she was always being left behind, ignored, left out. Apprehen-sion and suspicion in the elderly have often been dismissed as a response to their current helpless condition.

The rest of us also feel left behind, ignored, or left out some-times, but we're able to govern these feelings better, to subject them to reason's judgment. And it behooves us to do this. Because when the brain can no longer filter its emotions through reason, when the past is lost, they can emerge as wak-ing nightmares.

Another tenet of validation therapy advocates affirming the damaged person's current reality instead of pointing out its fac-tual inconsistencies and discrepancies.

In other words, I shouldn't say to my mother, "You can't pos-sibly have seen Grady this morning, Mother. He lives a thou-sand miles away." Such insistence on logic had little effect on my mother, except to make her more agitated, so I decided to try the validation mode on one of those afternoons when she steadfastly shut her eyes and refused to speak to me. She was often like this after I had been away a day or more.

"I think you must be angry because I wasn't here yesterday, Mother," I begin. (According to validation theory, you're supposed to help them put into words the feelings they might not have the capacity to articulate.)

She turns her head to stare out the window.

"I can understand that," I go on. "You must get lonely."

"You always do that to me," she mutters now, almost too low for me to hear.

My own nerves are on edge, and I feel like making an angry defense of myself. But the validation instructions say not to take what they say personally. So I bite my lip and take a deep breath.

This pause is propitious because it gives her time to embark on a rambling tale I can scarcely follow, the characters being only hazy pronouns and the setting unspecified.

"It was time to come to the table," my mother says, "but I couldn't because I wasn't finished yet. She got mad at me and this other girl. But I just went on working and kept my mouth shut."

I sit back and let my breath out slowly. "How did that make you feel?" I asked, shuddering at this psycho-cliché.

She turns a frowning face toward me as if she finds the answer too obvious to need explanation.

Nevertheless, I put the words in her mouth. "I bet that feels bad, when you can't say what you want to."

She glances away again, but her lids flicker, no longer frozen stone. "You just say whatever pleases them," she says.

I stroke her forearm. "That's what you've always had to do, isn't it, Mother?"

"You just try to keep everyone happy," she says.

"Still," I say, my own anger dissipated now, "it doesn't feel good, does it? Having to hide what you really feel."

And at this, she sighs, lays her head on the pillow, and falls deeply asleep.

Just as my mother inhabited her metaphorical world, I groped for some analogy of my own that would make sense for me of what was happening inside her, what was happening between us. Sometimes I pictured her imprisoned in a fortress, say Russia's old Lubyanka Prison, while I stand outside, wondering if she is still alive inside its stone walls. That metaphor makes the self an embattled hero, bravely holding out against oppression.

Then there was the demon-possession analogy. In that one, the self resides within its own castle, which has been invaded by a hostile force. While such a metaphor acknowledged her suffering, it also implied a certain weakness in the castle's defenses. Was it structurally faulty, poorly designed? Had its defects made it vulnerable to attack? Or had a betrayer allowed the enemy within its walls?

On the other side of the glass doors that blocked off the Alzheimer's wing at Fair Acres a woman stands and cries "Help me! Help me!" without letup for hours on end. This naked fear of abandonment unsettles both the other residents and their visitors. Was this fear a new development, the result of the woman's institutionalization, or had it always lurked within? Now that the ramparts of reason have been breached, have her demons escaped or have they invaded? I don't know. I can't say. It troubles me.

How are we to find the most precise picture, the perfect figure, to accurately describe where the self is located within the visible flesh and how it gets trapped or lost or buried there?

The Hebrew Bible tells us that God exhaled his own breath to animate mortal flesh. The Quakers say we carry an eternal flame inside us. Both images are pleasant enough when things are going well, but what of someone in my mother' shape? What happened to her inner light? Had it been doused, smothered, stamped out? If so, by what infernal darkness? Or is God's own breath slowly leaking out through the fissures in her brain? What then of this limp balloon we're left to deal with?

While he was waiting to be executed, Socrates consoled his grieving disciples with the notion that the soul is immortal. Not only would his spirit keep on living after his body died, but it had existed even before he was conceived, a snippet of the eternal Ideal Being having somehow gotten snagged on a twig of Time.

This scrap of soul, he taught, making the best of a bad situation, merely uses the human body "as an instrument of perception." "Once ensnared, the soul," he maintained, is "dragged by the body into the region of the changeable, and wanders and is confused; the world spins round her, and she is like a drunkard."

Only by concentrating itself into a little ball of reflection can the soul exert any control over the body. If a soul keeps as much distance as possible between itself and its sensory instruments, it may escape from its temporary entanglement in time unmarred. Any soul that "draws after her no bodily taint," remains pure, Socrates counsels, because it has "always been engaged in the practice of dying."

Maybe his students found this argument convincing. Maybe Socrates even believed it himself. But then he only had to take a quick swig of hemlock; he didn't have to face years of slow, humiliating disintegration.

The world indeed spins round my mother, and she wanders, confused. But try as she might, she could not, at this point, roll her soul up into a tidy ball of reflection. Socrates may have been a brave man, but I don't think he knew squat about the practice of protracted dying.

His countryman, Aristotle, tutor to the young Alexander the Great, looked at our predicament through the opposite end of the telescope. Knowledge comes not from navel-gazing, he said, but precisely its contrary—world-gazing. Ignoring Socrates' warning about getting tangled up in messy matter, he gathered as many details about the natural world as he could assemble and spent his life organizing them into categories.

When Alexander the Great made his expedition to the East, he sent back plant and animal specimens for his old tutor's collections. Aristotle concluded that each self is unique, individual, and comes into existence at the same time as the body.

The soul he defined as "the essential 'whatness of a body.'"

"Suppose" he says, "the eye were an animal—then sight would have been its soul." But if an eye loses its sight, then it is no longer an actual eye, any more than the painted eye of a statue. Aristotle acknowledges that his definition may leave certain questions unanswered. Yet despite its inadequacies, that rough sketch of the soul's nature is the best we can do, he concludes in his matter-of-fact way. (All Aristotle's facts were of matter.)

I assimilated Aristotle's methodology, taking reams of notes as the months at the nursing home stretched into years. I liked his definition as well as his methodology. My mother's "essential whatness," however little remained accessible to me, was what I tried to touch each day I was with her.

Maybe it's true that some dementia patients undergo personality shifts so severe that their loved ones no longer recognize them as the people they were, but that had not happened with us. My mother was definitely *less* than she had been, but she had not become something else, a foreign creature altogether.

I kept talking to my mother's "essential whatness," even when I was not sure it could still hear me, buried as it was under the rubble of her detonated brain. That is the metaphor that came to me most often then. The federal building in Oklahoma City had been blown up the year before I returned to Texas to care for my mother, and those images had imprinted themselves on my memory. Added to those scenes were the earthquakes in Japan and Turkey and then the mudslides in Honduras. My imagination had plenty of material to work with.

Most victims of those disasters died immediately. But a few lingered for days, even for miraculous weeks. As I pondered those pictures of devastation, I resolved that, even should my mother no longer be able to talk at all or to make those small gestures by which I recognized her best, even if she should go so far away in her mind that she no longer recognized me, all my care would be for that essential whatness, buried under the rubble.

For however long it took after the earthquake, survivors stayed with their loved ones, squatting by the wreckage. They kept talking to the buried people even after they could no longer hear a response, letting them know they were still there. Because leaving people to die alone, even for the poor and help-less, is unthinkable.

13

Thanksgiving at Fair Acres

When I was a teenager my church youth group would make an annual Christmas pilgrimage to what people then called the "old folks home." We took small wrapped gifts, perhaps a comb and bottle of shaving lotion for men, handkerchiefs and hand cream for women. Our youth leader did all the cheery talking. We only had to sing and grin. The more virtuous or socially skilled among us might shake a few of the clawlike hands or pat several bony shoulders. The rest of us just sang carols, crowding around the bedside of strangers while we exchanged sidelong glances, letting one another know we understood this wasn't real, that we had no personal connection to all this creepy weirdness. As soon as we could, we escaped into the cold night air outside, our pent breath exploding in blasts of laughter.

I was not one of the better people. I dreaded these nursing home excursions, and not merely because of the sensory and metaphysical assaults aging flesh inflicts on the young. Even at fifteen, I knew that we were putting on an act, performing—in all the permutations of that word's meaning—our Christian duty.

For the most part, we had no idea who these deplorable figures were in their wheelchairs and sickbeds. We weren't even curious. The season demanded charity the way it demanded colored lights, and we provided it, or at least its ceremony. We sang at the nursing homes to warm ourselves with the glow of our own virtue in the same way we Texans use angel hair and tinsel icicles to work up a fake nostalgia for snowy Christmas landscapes.

As an adult, I made a few visits to elderly relatives or friends in nursing homes, but my next significant exposure came in Wyoming twenty-two years later. We had just moved to a new town and, having a lot of free time on my hands, I decided to volunteer at a VA hospital two afternoons a week. By then I was old enough myself to be curious about old people. A number of important people in my life were nearing eighty. I was beginning to face the fact that they might get seriously sick or even die some day. What would that be like?

From the patients, mostly veterans of World Wars I and II, I got an introductory course on amputation, lung cancer, and stroke. Wheeling patients to the radiology lab or physical therapy, I observed their gauze-wrapped stumps, nicotine-yellowed nails, colostomy bags. Most were men, and fitness had not been a concept, much less a priority, for them. They would sit on the side of their beds, wheezing with emphysema or struggling to drag a recognizable word from under the avalanche of a stroke-damaged brain. A few would talk, but most were sunk in the silence that comes either from illness or living alone too long.

When my circumstances changed and I was no longer able to volunteer at the hospital, I found I missed those afternoons pushing wheelchairs. They had introduced me to a world I now could see was not only real but one with which I did indeed have some personal connection. Still, I was glad that none of my elderly relatives were living in such a place. To my knowledge, none ever had. Nor, I was certain then, would my parents.

The first couple of months I came through Fair Acres's dark mahogany doors, inset with etched glass, I had been disgusted by the irony of the foyer, masquerading as a sedate, upscale hotel. Muted light from brass lamps fell on a silk flower arrangement atop the cherry wood sideboard in the foyer. But the Ethan Allen attempt at elegance disappears as soon as you pass the portal to the hallway. Along the corridors where the residents live, the understated lighting gives way to fluorescent overhead panels, the carpet to vinyl tile studded here and there with fold-up yellow signs warning of wet floors.

During those early days after my mother's move here, I would sail past the nurse's station, scanning to my right the bedraggled but still ambulatory crew occupying the waterproof Queen Anne chairs in the communal living room. Though the furniture is arranged to form a circle in the hope of fostering fellowship, the attempt is vain. The residents do not talk to one another. The only human voice comes from a portable radio belonging to a resident who keeps it tuned to Christian talk shows.

To my left a ring of wheelchairs circles the nurse's station like beleaguered pioneer wagons. These are occupied by residents who generally require closer supervision—the rockers, the weepers, those who must be kept from falling out of their chairs by Lap Buddies, padded cushions the staff are careful never to call "restraints." (Certain words, like "patients" are forbidden here. Everyone is a "resident.") A few in the ring of wheelchairs simply prefer that location to the living room, probably because there's more action at the nurse's station. There, phones ring, the staff banters or complains among themselves, family members stop to make inquiries or requests. Despite the activity, however, the wheelchair people around the nurse's station, like their ambulatory counterparts in the living room area, appear completely oblivious to the person next to them. They don't talk to or even look at one another, except on rare occasions. Their faces are as expressionless as Easter Island monoliths. Several doze. A couple of faces are twisted in some private anguish. One woman clutches a stuffed rabbit. Another moans monotonously "Help me, help me." The rest stare resolutely ahead in stony, almost regal, detachment.

Only when visitors cross the expanse of the rotunda do they shift their gaze, glancing up at the alien outsiders, some of whom smile at them with determined, facile cheer. The look they receive in return accuses: "Don't think you're doing us any favor. You're not getting off the hook that easy."

After the first few weeks of running this daily gauntlet, I had started speaking to some of the people I passed on the way to my mother's room. By then I had scoped out the ones I thought might respond. But none returned my greeting, at least at first. A few looked up with a dazed frown, as if I had startled them from deep reverie. One or two, after a second's hesitation, gave me a single nod or at least met my gaze directly.

I didn't blame the ones who ignored me. They had every right to their withdrawal. Only a handful of residents have visitors who come on even a weekly basis. More are visited occasionally, some rarely or never. People who've been abandoned develop a thick coat of defensive frost.

Over the course of a couple of weeks, I struck up an acquaintance with a woman I passed every day. At first, she only looked up when I spoke to her. Then a few days later, she nodded. By the end of the week, she was returning my greeting. Now, as soon as she sees me, certain expectancy suffuses her face and she lifts her hands to catch mine between them.

"These hands is too cold," she tells me, shaking her head. "You need to warm up."

Stella is tiny—eighty pounds at most—and has the same well-defined features as a great aunt who lived with my family when I was growing up. Her lips sink over her toothless gums and her chin juts sharply like a bowsprit. Her left leg has been amputated at the knee, and her right foot, usually shod in a red flat, is positioned neatly on the wheelchair's single footrest. I have no idea how she lost the other leg. Maybe one day I'll feel I can ask. She has a wardrobe of four or five dresses, with which I am now quite familiar. Something, probably some special care she takes to straighten her sleeve or smooth her skirt over her lap, prompts me to compliment her frequently on her appearance. On special occasions like today—the Family Thanksgiving Dinner—she wears a string of red beads.

Viola, who lives on Two Hundred Hall, refuge of the more

independent residents, is not planning to attend the Family Thanksgiving Dinner. Not many residents from that wing will. They are the establishment's upper crust, people who could conceivably function well at home but who, for one reason or another, have washed up on the shores of Fair Acres. Most have physically debilitating diseases like severe diabetes or MS, but remain in full control of their mental faculties. They form their own private club, playing cards in the activity room during the afternoon or visiting one another in their immoderately decorated rooms.

Viola has lovely shoulder-length white hair, expertly waved in the manner of a 1940s movie star. Disabled by a bad heart, she, along with her cancer-riddled husband, moved to Fair Acres together the day after they sold their home in a coastal city a hundred miles east of here. He died last week.

She tells me about it, sitting in her wheelchair, parked in the doorway of her room, careful to assure me that she was fully prepared for the loss, welcomed it, in fact, "for his sake."

She tells me my husband stopped to pray with her a few days ago. "He's such a dear. But," she shakes her head, "I'm fine." She makes a graceful, deprecating movement with her hand, brushing the front of her duster.

Her husband's empty bed, I notice, has already been filled with a new resident. Viola looks up with a wry smile. "My new roommate complains that I have too many visitors." She gestures to the other rooms down the corridor where her visitors live—all of them in-house.

My husband has also made friends with Elsie, another Two Hundred Hall resident, but one who, strangely enough, prefers to spend her days in the wagon train circling the nurse's station. Elsie is a retired schoolteacher whose son, she has confided to David, brought her to Huntsville after she'd had a stroke and installed her in Fair Acres. Now the son never comes to see her. He apparently leaves that duty to his wife, a tall blonde who owns the health club where I swim.

Elsie is a tall woman, or at least she would be if she could still stand. You can tell because her useless left leg, elevated on her wheelchair's footrest to improve circulation, juts out into the traffic lane around the nurse's station. Elsie sleeps a good bit of the time, holding a washcloth to one side of her face to catch the saliva that flows from her stroke-slackened mouth. Her former schoolteacher speech is slurred now as if she'd been on an all-night binge. Nevertheless, her conversation retains its acerbic humor and no-nonsense flavor. Today, she is already parked at a table when my father and I wheel my mother into the dining room. Her aerobic daughter-in-law sits at her side, looking slightly dazed.

Today is not really Thanksgiving, of course. We're only pretending. In fact, that holiday is more than a week away, though in nursing-home-time a week more or less doesn't make much difference. I don't even attempt to explain this to my mother. The abstractions of time are beyond her now. Nor do I mention that, next week, my husband and I will be eating our "real" Thanksgiving dinner in Kansas with our daughters' families.

My mother, fortunately, has bought this innocent subterfuge about the date; she's dressed in her newest dress and some obliging aide has smudged her cheeks with blush as well as dabbing on a touch of lipstick. Unfortunately, however, the excitement of the occasion is already threatening to overwhelm her. Her eyes are darting about the room, trying to sort out the unaccustomed hubbub. Her breath comes in short, shallow snatches.

The tables have been rearranged, end to end pilgrim-style, for the Thanksgiving feast, so my father and I sit on either side of my mother while cousin Margaret takes a place at the end of the table.

Across from us sit Norman, whose disabilities are clearly genetic, and James, a dark man in a Mister Rogers cardigan who moves with glacial stateliness to compensate for his halting, stroke-damaged gait. Both men are living room regulars. James's usual outpost is the Queen Anne loveseat along the north wall. Norman is the owner of the Christian music boom box. They maintain the same distant reserve today that they display on non-holidays.

"May we join you?" I ask, as we pull out our chairs, making my voice bright with what I hope they will see as holiday cheer. James inclines his head in a courtly manner. Norman says, "Sure," and blinks several times in what appears to be welcome. "Isn't this nice," I say enthusiastically, gesturing toward the centerpieces—baskets of orange, yellow, and red silk leaves, accented with stalks of dried grass and little ears of plastic corn. James nods; Norman says, "Yes, nice." My father grins encouragingly. Margaret says, "Ooh, yes."

My mother, however, is still panting, the breath, rapid and shallow, coming through her nose in faint wheezes. I take her hand and, turning my over-bright social tone down a notch, point out the centerpieces to her. She points instead to a large basket of rolls, slowly growing cold on the table. I butter one and give it to her.

Meanwhile, an aide is maneuvering another wheelchair into position across the table from my father. In it is a woman who looks much older than my mother, even though her permed hair is rust-colored and her silk blouse immaculate. Her head shakes like Katharine Hepburn's, and she clutches a washcloth in one hand with which she continually dabs at her mouth. The washcloth, I see, is to mop up saliva pushed toward the front of her mouth by her tongue, which squirms compulsively, like some small burrowing animal.

"You're joining us," I say. "How nice." I introduce the members of our little party. Beaming, my father half rises and extends his hand across the table. The woman shakes it loosely and, after dabbing at her mouth, tells us her name, which, after several repetitions, I finally make out as Mary. My mother's panting has slowed a little, and she nods shyly at the woman.

I search for a conversational gambit that might spin some fine thread of connection, some link of sympathy between us across the table. Margaret, whose high, thin voice can scarcely be heard above the dining room hubbub, pitches in too. I feel like an old-fashioned telephone operator, plugging an array of lines into a decrepit switchboard.

Mary struggles to respond with appropriate chitchat, drawing from her own store of social pleasantries. Judging from Mary's unstained silk bosom and her newly manicured, glossy red nails, I figure she must come from the exclusive neighborhood of Two Hundred Hall.

Leaving Mary to Margaret, I concentrate on shouting inanities loud enough to be heard across the table by Norman and James.

"Smell that? Mm. Turkey!"

"What kind of pie are you going to have? Pumpkin or pecan?"

"Want a roll to tide you over?"

From time to time I nod encouragingly at my father who, in any case, can't hear over the bustle and clatter of food being brought from the kitchen and laid out, buffet-style.

In all, it takes a good forty minutes to get all the people and the food to the tables. By the time the director quiets everyone to say grace, my mother has long ago consumed the roll I buttered for her and is listing acutely leftward like a rag doll in her chair. As soon as Judy, the activities director with a bullhorn voice, announces the logistics of the serving line, I make a break for the buffet table to fill a plate for my mother. James and Norman are right behind me. I load a plate with turkey, dressing, gravy, sweet potatoes, fruit salad, cranberry sauce—the dishes I know my mother has always liked. And after I put the plate in front of her and begin to cut the turkey into bite-sized morsels, I name over its contents, hoping to coax her appetite.

"Take a bite of the dressing, Mother, you'll like it."

She ignores me, making her way slowly but steadily through the turkey I've cut into small pieces.

"Would you like another roll? I'll butter it for you."

She shakes her head and, after the turkey, puts down her fork, leaving the rest of the meal untouched. The noise, I know, distracts her, the sounds a jumble she can't sort into meaning.

"Dessert?" I urge. "I think there's pumpkin pie. Or would you like cobbler?" She doesn't answer, but I get her a small piece of pumpkin. She ignores it and begins to pant again.

As soon as my father has finished, I suggest he leave for his afternoon nap. Then I wheel my mother back to her room. I close her door, and we're both relieved by the quiet that settles around us there. I press the call button for the aides to come and lift her into bed, then sit beside her, holding her hand until she drops into a fitful sleep.

"It went well, don't you think?" I whisper to Margaret when she tiptoes in a few minutes later to say goodbye. I'm feeling that sappy self-satisfaction of a hostess who has just successfully pulled off a big dinner party.

I'm even more pleased the next day when James, for the first time, returns my wave from his post on the Queen Anne loveseat, lifting his index finger and smiling, tentatively as though taking a social risk, hoping I remember him.

I regret, of course, that my mother hadn't derived much real pleasure from the event, that her excitement peaked too soon, leaving her limp and isolated at the Thanksgiving table. I have to fight back the guilt that arises from enjoying anything she can't. And even when I sidestep the guilt, my grief for her whose joys are so circumscribed threatens to engulf even my pleasure at everyone else's enjoyment.

But the truth was, I felt happy. And I don't think it came entirely from the smug gratification of knowing James and Norman had gotten a sliver of conversation along with their turkey and pumpkin pie. Or that Mary, probably a social powerhouse in her day, got to wow us once more with her classy blouse and fingernails.

Pleased to meet you, people say in Texas when they're introduced. And I was immeasurably pleased, finally, to have met them all. I hope they were pleased as well. My own pleasure came from their having let me in through a crack in their carefully constructed indifference. Through that crack I caught a glimpse of the other side of the wall, the one I had fled in my teenage fear and hubris. The other side of the wall where I will live some day.

"How did the dinner at the nursing home go?" my daughter asked me the following week as we were recovering in her living room from the "real" Thanksgiving dinner.

"You know that parable in Luke where the master sends his servant out to the highways and hedges to bring in the maimed, the halt, and the blind after the people he'd invited to the banquet don't show up?"

"Mmm . . . I think I remember."

"Well, that's how it was. I got to come to the banquet too."

14

The Hour of Our Death

Ever since she got to be the age I am now, my mother talked about how she was ready to die, was even eager for the joys—and rest—of heaven, about how she didn't understand why some people put up such a fight when their time came.

But, after a year in the nursing home, my mother changed her mind, what was left of it. She decided she didn't want to die yet. She was very clear on that point, despite her confusion about everything else. And, during that first year at Fair Acres, I came to see that she was right. She wasn't ready yet.

I had always agreed with my mother's earlier position. My own favorite metaphor for death was setting out on a great voyage of discovery, with the excitement and anticipation such adventures afford. In my mind's eye, the ship on which I embark on this journey is a sleek sailing craft whose canvases billow and crack in the freshening wind.

Watching my mother not want to die may change this metaphor for me. Even if I keep the voyage motif, I'm likely to downgrade the picture of my outward-bound craft to a small outrigger canoe with its bamboo float broken off.

After months of wondering why the topic of her death had disappeared from her screen, I decided it was time we had a serious conversation about death. I have, after all, read the books urging you not to put this off. People who are dying often want desperately to talk about their approaching end, they say, but clam up because of their family's discomfort with the topic.

Before I raised the issue, however, I consulted a friend who is a hospital chaplain and another who is certified in spiritual formation. Yes, they agreed. This is something that needs to happen, something positive you can do for your mother. Okay, I thought, at least I won't fail her in this particular area.

So I arrived at the nursing home one afternoon, loins girded for talking about death. Not that I had any special reason to worry. My mother was not a squeamish person. She still talked about bodily functions even then without reserve. Besides, I had the precedence of all those earlier conversations we'd had before her illness when we had both agreed that, while dying might not be a pleasant prospect, the state of being dead held few fears for us. In fact, it wasn't death at all, but a fuller life.

My mother envisioned the afterlife primarily as a giant family reunion. Her vision of the future was easier to talk about than my own version which involved the more mystical aspects of the speed of light and quantum leaps. While my mother had not talked about her dinner-on-the-grounds heaven in a good while, she had continued to make comments like "I might as well die" or, more frequently, "I'm so weary of all this." So I figured there was nothing to keep me from approaching the subject head on.

"Do you think much about dying, Mother?" I asked her that afternoon. The weather had finally turned cool enough in September to wheel her outside onto the little patio tucked away by the front entrance. I poured part of a Coke over crushed ice for her and was drinking the rest from the can myself.

She blinked and swiveled her head to look at me. "Not especially," she said.

I should have taken the hint then, but, duty-bound, I

pressed on, deciding to back up and ease into the subject by the pragmatism route.

"Do you have two burial plots or just one at Oakwood?" Oakwood is the cemetery where most of her family is buried.

"Two," she said. She swiveled her head back around to stare at the flag a breeze was beginning to lift.

I waited, but she didn't add anything to that. Having come this far, however, I didn't want to abandon the effort quite yet. I cast about in my mind for another scrap of practicality.

"So . . . what would you like to be buried in?"

She stared at me again, frowning. "Something . . . ," she gestured vaguely, "well, not rags."

I chuckled uneasily. "I don't intend to do that. I just thought you might have a preference. I mean, would you like a dress or a suit better?"

She appeared to consider this thoughtfully—she was having a particularly "up" day brainwise—as if it were a question of attending an important social function. Which I suppose it is.

"It's getting cooler," she reflected tentatively.

Picking up this clue, I press on. "So it is. Yes. So I take it you'd like a suit then because that would be warmer?"

She nods, seems satisfied with this extrapolation of her remark on the weather.

I refrain from pointing out the absurdity of her cold, dead body needing the extra warmth of a wool suit jacket. In earlier times I would have. She always prided herself in facing facts, especially hard ones, a value she taught me. Today I'm simply pleased she's noticed the change in season.

Whatever satisfaction I may have taken in having done my psychological duty was shot down the following week, however.

It is not a good day. She is in bed, having refused to go to the dining room for lunch. I have been sitting by her bedside for a half-hour, trying to make conversation, but she keeps her eyes resolutely on the scene outside her window, refusing all my usual conversational gambits. Then suddenly, with unwonted clarity and bitterness, she says, "You just want me to die anyway."

"What?" I splutter. "I never said any such thing."

"You're already talking about my funeral."

After a fatal moment of hesitation I say, "I only asked because I needed to know. About the burial plots and what you wanted to wear."

"But I never—" I break off the protest, overcome with confusion. The old childhood fear of being caught out by my mother bubbles up like swamp gas. My voice sounds unconvincing, even to my own ears. Because she is onto me, at least to some undeniable, if small, part of me.

Nevertheless, she looks a bit abashed herself now, as if she really might have gone too far, accused me of too much or too unjustly. She fumbles for a word.

"Different. Dingle. That boy."

It takes me several seconds to untangle that word puzzle. Remembering that my daughter and her four-year-old son had visited a few days earlier, I suggest his name. "Dylan?"

"Yes. I looked at that little boy and I thought, 'I'm not going to die.'" She hammers each word home separately and distinctly, like a ten-penny nail. It sounds like a line from a victory-over-disease movie.

What can I do but make an affirming noise, yet, for a second time, I feel the guile rise in me. Because she is going to die. It has taken me two years to admit this, and has been, without doubt, the hardest fact I've ever had to face.

Elisabeth Kübler-Ross did us all a big favor when she shone her little flashlight onto our culture's dark secret—the way we conspire to deny that, despite all the evidence to the contrary, we will die. We don't so much refuse to believe this bald, irrefutable fact as not admit it to our consciousness for consideration. I am convinced the media could do us a big favor by broadcasting this public service announcement every thirty minutes: *Remember. You die.*

For at least a year after my mother's Parkinson's disease was diagnosed, she would periodically declare with a triumphant lift of her chin that Jesus was coming soon. Unstated but clearly implied was the claim that this final act in the history of the world would occur before her own death, indeed before the disease reduced her to a pitiable heap of flaccid flesh.

Such desperation was unlike her. Whenever she made these proclamations, this woman who taught me the value of facing facts, I would stare at her a moment, startled by this embarrassing exploitation of her own fortitude and faith. Then I would look away. How do you point out to someone facing a future as grim as hers that she's kidding herself, pulling the wool over her own eyes? Her conscience would never allow her to wish for a global catastrophe like a nuclear holocaust. For her, it had to be the second coming—the ultimate happy ending.

During her five years at Fair Acres, such predictions or even desires gradually faded from her conversation. Jesus, it appeared, had already tarried too long to do her any earthly good. Maybe this was the reason she no longer mentioned him at all.

Nevertheless, she was still not ready to give this life up. She continued to cling. She got depressed and weary, even at times expressed those feelings, but she wasn't ready to turn loose yet. Whenever I brought up loved ones she believed were waiting for her in heaven—her father, her sisters, the aunt who gave her whatever mothering she got—she would turn her head away, as if signaling a certain impatience with my attempt at consolation.

Her disinterest in the religious ramifications of death came as an even greater surprise to me than her recoil from hard facts. After all, faith had been her only means of facing the facts, so many of them hard and bitter, that gnarled her life like oak galls. Yet she was loath even to take the name of her creator or her savior on her lips. Why? What became of the spiritual strength that sustained her through an unrewarding marriage, unrealized dreams, and the ache of her own losses? She seemed to have put it away somewhere and forgotten where she laid it.

No, worse than that. She didn't appear to want to find it. She frowned at any religious reference, as if you had thrust a photograph of a stranger before her and demanded that she identify the person. And this—the amputation of her spiritual sensibility—was, I confess, a fact I had a hard time facing. Didn't she love God any more, I wondered? I'm pretty sure she no longer trusted him.

Once, during her third year at Fair Acres, she seemed to be sinking rapidly for a couple of days. She lay turned onto her right side, her knees drawn up. She barely opened her eyes when I tried to rouse her. I lowered the side rail on her bed and sat down beside her, taking her hand in mine.

"I've been thinking about my brothers and sisters," she says in a low voice. "You heard about Betty going off from us."

Her sister Betty was only an infant when their mother died. *Gone off from us*, I sense, is code for "died."

"No, Mother," I put in, still insisting on accuracy. "Betty's at home in Conroe." I name over her siblings, living and dead, in order, trying to engage her in listing them. But she seems disinterested, as though I had missed the point.

She asks for water but is too weak either to hold the glass or guide the straw to her lips. "Don't leave," she says as I settle her on the pillow again.

"I'm not. Don't worry," I say. "Are you scared?"

"No." But after a moment she adds in a tone as clear as water and innocent of self-deception, "Just at night. I don't want to be alone. I want someone with me." She looks at me and says again, "Don't leave me."

Her eyes drift shut and I think she's sleeping, but, after a few moments she says, "We had our hands tied together, remember?"

"Like prisoners?" I ask. "Do you feel like a prisoner, Mother?"

She gives an impatient little shake of her head against the pillow. "We were walking up a trail to heaven. Our hands . . ."

"Holding hands," I supply.

This seems to satisfy her. "I was holding your hand." She opens her eyes and looks into mine. "You promised."

I have lain in bed many a night and, in the solitary dark, put the question to myself: *Do* I want her to die?

Yes and no.

I tried to imagine how it would happen, devised a number of scenarios, most of which involve the phone ringing in the middle of the night.

Mrs. Owens?

Yes? What is it? Is it my mother?

I'm afraid so.

I had in fact gotten two calls from the nursing home, both around seven in the morning, telling me the ambulance had taken her to the hospital, both times for minor strokes. So I know how the heart races and every object takes on hard, bright edges. I have experienced the way the mind shifts into hyperdrive, operates with such exceptional efficiency it leaves you dizzy at the door of the emergency room. You wear serenity like a shield to keep your panic from infecting others till the crisis eases.

After that point though, my imagination faltered. On some unforeseen but quite specific date in the future, when the final crisis comes, would there still be light to see, air to breathe?

I used to sit by her bed while she slept and watch for her chest to rise and fall, praying to be with her at the end so she would be less afraid. So I would finally know . . . what?

At times it would strike me quite forcefully that when she goes, this mad woman curled in the hospital bed, then I could have my real mother back, or at least my memory of her. The real her.

At the same time, I found myself highly incensed last night at a comment I heard a college student make about his aged grandmother. "She doesn't know who I am," he said with a snort. "I don't even bother to correct her anymore. She was married to my grandfather for sixty-four years and she can't remember that he's dead." His voice is heavy with disgust. "I figure when a person ceases to change, they're already dead."

I wanted to smack him. I presume he meant "progress," not "change." Mistaking your grandson or misplacing your husband *is* change, just not for the better. But to say the woman is *dead?* That's just another way of not facing facts.

Enormous chunks of my mother broke off and disappeared, like floes from a melting iceberg. Her physical presence, however disfigured and dismaying, was still her. It was not some discardable pizza box.

Nevertheless, it hurts to watch someone you love die, especially if it takes a long time. As they change, so do you. And for better or worse, who can tell? The thought takes root in the darkness of your heart: She will never get well, never again be the person she was. Can nothing I do help? Wouldn't it be merciful simply to end this suffering?

But whose suffering—hers or mine?

When you share someone's suffering, I've learned, there's no clean division between the parts. Here's yours, here's mine. It's more like Br'er Rabbit and the tar baby. The harder you struggle to escape misery's sticky grip, the more it clings to you.

It's easy to see how his grandmother's shrinking self offends the college student. For him, young and with widening horizons, change has always meant more, not less. He has a hard time imagining life as a contracting sphere; so far he's only known an expanding universe. As the song says, he hasn't got time for the pain.

At least he has the excuse of youth. But the rest of us, whose bodies are undeniably diminishing, can all too easily imagine ourselves in the place of the shriveling figure in the bed. At fifty-eight, my physical powers have undeniably begun shutting down. The power to conceive a child, to regenerate my optic nerves, to play Bach—all gone.

Today I found a note I'd written on a scrap of paper two years ago in the middle of the night and later stuck in my journal. "Mother's fears are no different from my own," it read, "except in degree. We're both afraid of the dark."

I've had enough experience trying to extricate myself from the tar baby's gummy embrace to know that the pain and the person cannot be separated. To free myself from one means ridding myself of the other.

I became acutely aware of just how hard it is to divide the pain between us the day I signed my mother's admission papers for the nursing home. A year earlier, spurred on by my father's approaching heart surgery, both my parents had signed a "living will," otherwise known as a "directive to physicians." The document instructed that, in the event "life-sustaining procedures would serve only to artificially postpone the moment of my death," those procedures be withheld or withdrawn, and that "I be permitted to die naturally."

A second document, "Durable Power of Attorney for Health Care," designated me as the agent "to make any and all health care decisions" for both my parents. I had driven them to their church one sunny February afternoon so that the church secretary could sign as witness to these documents. Afterward I drove them to their bank where we put the originals in their safety deposit box.

The nursing home's version of "Directive to Physicians," however, was much more detailed than the simple form originally witnessed by the church secretary.

The day I signed it, I was sitting at a table in the conference room of the nursing home. Coordinating the handoff of my mother from the hospital rehab center to the nursing home had been harder than I anticipated. It was only ten-thirty in the morning, but already I felt daunted.

I had already filled plastic bags with her clothes and packed boxes with toilet articles, plastic bedpans and wash basins, padded heel protectors, wheelchair peripherals, flower vases, and potted plants.

In addition, the protocols of transferring my mother from one facility to the other were as intricate as high-level diplomatic negotiations. Both agencies take care to demarcate where their legal liabilities begin and end. During all these procedures, I had to keep explaining to my mother in terms that will let her down gently, that she's going to a place, the name of which strikes terror into every person's heart—a nursing home. At the same time, I tried to keep my father's damaged and agitated heart from running away with him.

Already he and I have signed a number of papers at the long conference table. The table is dark and highly polished. On one side sit my father and I, on the other a staff secretary and a large, dark, authoritative woman in a white lab coat whose name tag reads, improbably, Daisy Blossom. I am not certain just what position she occupies at the nursing home. She jokes that she's done just about every job there during her decade-long tenure.

She peers at us over half-glasses as she passes us page after page of official notifications and forms to sign or initial. Of course, there is no time to actually read them. Daisy's deep voice is simultaneously funny, reassuring, and indisputable. A new secretary is being trained to handle records; from time to time she creeps back into the room to ask Daisy nervous questions, but Daisy never loses her cool.

My father is often near tears.

Finally, Daisy hands us a document with multiple pages and explains that we must check off which of the steps in "life-sustaining procedures" we do not want them to take. My father is beginning to crumble under the strain of struggling to hear, to understand, to decide. I'm certain this particular document will be his final undoing, so I take it from Daisy and glance over it.

At the top of the list of life-sustaining procedures are the ones you expect, the kind involving electronic devices with beeping monitors you see in movies. Machines that artificially stimulate the heart to beat or the lungs to breathe. I instantly check that one. Then the choices get harder. Feeding tubes in the event the patient is unable to swallow. Ventilators. Artificial breathing devices.

Does this mean oxygen tanks? Surely not. You see people in supermarkets hauling around their portable green cylinders. After hesitating, I check those too.

But the easy choices end there. "Life sustaining medica-tions." Chemotherapy, antibiotics, intravenous drips. Blood transfusion, tracheotomy, intubation. I suddenly don't know what to do, what I want. What she would want.

Until that moment, thoughts about my own dying had run something like this: Okay, so you know you're going to die someday. And though you're willing to cooperate with possible cures for most diseases that might strike you, some diseases are either incurable or the cure at some point becomes worse than the alternative. You have a right, maybe even a duty, to accept the inevitable and refuse more treatment. At that point, you may as well depart this life with whatever dignity is left you.

This doesn't mean active suicide. Just the option to say "No thanks, I've had enough. Don't try to help me any more."

My mother had seen both a younger sister and her closest

friend die of cancer after agonizing chemotherapy. She didn't want that, she had told me. Why hang on for a few more desperate, depleted months?

When I was a toddler, before technology made it possible to keep badly injured or desperately ill people alive, my eighty-year-old great-grandmother, blind and frail, had died at home. She simply refused to eat any longer, hiding the wads of food her daughter tried to get down her under the mattress.

At ninety-one, my mother's father broke his hip and refused to get up again following successful surgery to repair it. When he left the hospital, my mother brought him to her house to die, a feat he accomplished in less than two weeks. Given her family's inherent stubbornness in the face of death, I had expected that, following her own initial diagnosis, my mother would eventually dig in her heels and make up her mind to die. But I had reckoned without dementia.

The truth is she's no longer able to read or understand the list I sit staring at in the conference room. I close my eyes and see her sitting beside me on her front porch two summers ago, scanning with narrowed eyes the tops of the tall oaks for the mockingbird we can hear but not spot. "I just pray I don't lose my mind," she says. "I think I could bear anything but that."

The very condition she most feared had, in a final irony, defeated the famous familial willpower. The person she was the evening we watched for the mockingbird would reject the life of the person she was on the day I admitted her to the nursing home. But the person she was that morning could not choose what the earlier version surely would have. She was afraid, and could no longer fight against that fear.

Nor could I do it for her.

I could not bring myself to check off more than the top items on the list, despite what my mother might want if she were clear-headed. Instead, I go by what I believe my father would reasonably agree to, were he not so worn down that I dare not even read the list of choices to him.

I realize, of course, that this question of when and how life ought to end has no easy answer. In fact, it most likely has many

answers. Just like the meaning of life. Everyone's life means
something different. And we can't know what that is until it's
finished, complete. Sometimes not then. One thing I did know
was that the answer to my mother's end did not lie with me.

At times she would have what her cousin Margaret calls "spells."
They usually happened between noon and two o'clock. Several
times I arrived to find her clinging to the bed rails, her breath
coming fast and shallow. Her chin quivered and she appeared
to be sucking on her own tongue.

I sit down in the wheelchair beside her bed and take her
hand. "Mother? You okay?"

She takes a little gasp of air and puffs out "No."

"You want me to call the nurse?"

She shakes her head, gripping my hand. In her palm's fleshy
pad I can feel her pulse, always erratic, fluttering like a bird held
in your hand. I stroke her forearm gently, rhythmically. Slowly,
slowly, she begins to relax.

Once, after her panic had subsided, I asked, "Were you
afraid?"

She nods her head and closes her eyes.

"Were you afraid you were going to die?" This time I haven't
prepared the question; it just pops out. I very much want her
to say no.

But she nods again. I keep stroking her arm.

After a moment she opens her eyes, staring up at me as if
from the bottom of a deep hole. "I don't want to go away from
you," she says.

I kiss her forehead, wordless at this naked declaration of love
and need. A few months earlier I would have said, as if explaining death to a three-year-old, that she needn't be afraid, that she
won't be alone, she'll be with God. I've tried any number of
ways to find the switch that can flip on that steadfast faith she
had always relied on—along with willpower, of course—to get
her through the hard places in her life. The faith she had worked
her whole life to instill in me. I hadn't found that switch and I'd
pretty much given up fumbling for it.

I just kept running my fingers over the skin which is like oiled paper crimped across the long radius and ulna of her forearm, abashed to discover she loves me more than God.

But the day I signed the papers that would keep the doctor from sticking a plastic tube into my mother's stomach, it occurred to me that perhaps there was a second irony buried here beneath the surface of our condition. She was a broken person, yes. Her seemingly invincible self-control had dissolved in the chemical bath of her brain. All her difficult life long she relied on resolve to get her through the rough spots. Then that part of her had been—what? "Excised" implies too clean a procedure. At any rate, it wasn't there any more.

And who knows? Perhaps her steel-clad will had formed a barrier between her and God. When it was gone, when hard choices were too much to make and facts too hard to find, much less face, maybe then she would simply plop, defenseless, straight into the arms of Jesus.

The Last Chapter

After almost five years at Fair Acres, her body shutting down organ by organ, my mother died on St. Stephen's Day, the day after Christmas and the forty-fourth anniversary of my marriage. I do not intend to impose my words on her private death. I know that she would want a curtain drawn across that scene. In any case, my purpose here has been not to tell about the end but to describe an ending.

Not knowing the end is precisely the point of human death. Unlike the rest of the animal kingdom, we know it's coming and even a great deal these days about what causes it, but predicting the exact time or even the date eludes us. We plan our parenthood these days, plan for retirement, even plan our funerals, but the details of our death, short of suicide, remain outside our control. Rounding out this story of my mother's long goodbye, providing too much closure, would detract from that essential uncertainty.

Leon Wieseltier, in a memoir of the year following his own father's death, remarked on our current penchant for "closure." "What a ludicrous notion of emotional efficiency," he exclaims. "Americans really believe that the past is past." But the past,

Wieseltier reminds us, never really goes away; at most, he says, it "goes inside."

People I see interviewed on TV after some great calamity, often say they "just want to get on with their lives." The phrase has become one of our modern mantras. What do they mean, I wonder. What are they thinking? That life comes to us as a series of self-contained craft projects? There, that one's done, we say smartly, as we put away the scissors and paste—or the dead loved one. Time to move on to the next project.

But life, alas, is not art. Pictures have frames, the play ends with a final curtain, but life, as we say, goes on. And not in discrete episode-particles, but as a continuous wave.

I have written, not about death, which is certain, but about dying, which is an open, anxious space where we set up camp, unsure how long we'll be there. Learning how to die—or how to care for someone who is dying—means learning to live with not knowing what to do or when to do it. With not knowing how much longer, or even if, you can hold out. I live in time differently than I used to, floating along rather than swimming against the current.

The brain scientist Antonio Damasio has explored the connection between suffering and consciousness, a mystery that those who have a loved one afflicted by any kind of neurological deficit must ponder. In his book *The Feeling of What Happens,* Damasio studies what is going on in the brain when we feel happy or sad or angry or fearful. Different emotions, he discovered, are produced by different brain systems, most of them subcortical, the "unconscious" part of the brain.

Any organism, from a sea-urchin to a street urchin, responds to physical pain, whether or not it is a conscious being. That is, certain stimuli can induce a pattern of chemical and neural reactions in the organism.

Fortunately, we have learned how to block these chemical or neural pain pathways with analgesics, anesthetics, even hypnotism, in order to interrupt the flow of messages to the central nervous system, thus alleviating much of our experience of physical pain today.

Only conscious beings can "feel" emotional pain, however. To suffer, rather than just feel pain, you have to remember certain patterns from past events to which you have responded, and to call up those patterns internally. In other words, to imagine. This internal imaging then sets off the chain of chemical and neural patterns associated with those past events—worry, anticipation, disgust, longing. Each sort of emotion must access its own specific region of the brain in order for this imaging to take place, however.

Damasio's studies of people with certain kinds of brain damage have borne out his conclusions that consciousness is needed to feel emotion. One of Damasio's patients, a woman with akinetic mutism following a stroke, provides an example of the connection between consciousness and feeling. She had lain in something like a semi-coma for months, awake but unresponsive to any stimuli, including bright lights, loud noises, and appeals from her closest kin. Once in a while she would move her hand to pull up her blanket, but, other than regular waking and sleeping cycles, she showed no reaction to her environment.

Gradually, however, she emerged from this state, first by beginning to track moving objects with her eyes, then by responding to voices and faces, and finally by answering questions. Once she regained use of her faculties, she reported that she had felt no emotion at all during that time. She did not recognize anyone, did not attempt to focus her attention, indeed had no attention to focus. She did not feel resigned to her fate as she had no sense of wanting or desire. Nor did she have any sense of suffering from these deprivations.

This, says Damasio, is how people with advanced Alzheimer's disease also live in the world. As their attention, their awareness of the world, diminishes, their vacant stares accurately mirror their interior state. At any rate, this is what Damasio hopes for a friend of his, a well-known philosopher, now sunk in the final slough of Alzheimer's, a disease that may soon become the plague of the twenty-first century—the Living Black Death.

As my mother entered this stage of her descent, my only hope was that Damasio was right. If her brain, bit by bit, shut down the production of necessary electrochemicals and was damaged by ruptured blood supply lines, consciousness faltered and stuttered to a stop. What Damasio calls the "autobiographical self" no longer functioned. The suffering supposedly ceases.

Of course, all the evidence we've got to go on are the anecdotal accounts of people, such as his patient, who manage to struggle back from that far murky shore and regain consciousness. And the question still remains for the rest of us: How are we to relate to these disconnected loved ones?

Leon Wieseltier, not ordinarily an observant Jew, nevertheless decided to say Kaddish—the traditional prayer for the dead—when his father died. This was a considerable undertaking, since it involves attending a service at a synagogue every day for an entire year where the Kaddish is repeated following the daily Scripture reading and other prayers. He often longed for an end to the bother of getting up early and trudging through the early morning gloom to the prayer service. But one day as his year of obligation drew to a close, Wieseltier was shocked to discover that he had miscounted the days required. His responsibility would end the following day. Quite suddenly, nothing more was required of him. Instead of feeling relief, he wasn't so sure he was ready to be released from the obligation.

At times I also longed to be free of my seemingly interminable vigil. If only, I thought, I knew when to expect the end. But that hope was a delusion. If the end had come the next day, I would not have felt liberated from the excruciatingly slow, painful loosening of our ties. I still floundered about, bereft not only of my mother's shredded self, scarcely more than a memento then, but the steady pattern of my days. In some sense, I lost my mother long before her death. But I also lost what had given my life meaning for the previous five years.

Following his more or less solitary sojourn at Walden Pond, Thoreau wrote out his reasons for undertaking the experiment. "I went to the woods," he says, "because I wished to live deliberately, to front only the essential facts of life, and see if I could not learn what it had to teach, and not, when I came to die, discover that I had not lived."

One can indeed learn deep things from that world we've come to call "nature." It hums away, like some immense tuning fork, true to its internal character. Thoreau hoped to "live deep and suck all the marrow of life." He aimed to "shave close, to drive life into a corner, and reduce it to its lowest terms." Creation's single-mindedness appealed to Thoreau; the woods and the pond and the sky all did precisely and well exactly what they were meant to do.

By contrast, the unnatural world of human society, messy with complications, contradictions, and squandered energy, gave him misanthropic fits. He learned a lot at Walden, and we owe him a large debt of gratitude for passing on those lessons, which, of course, we honor more in the breach than the observance.

But now a four-lane highway skirts Walden Pond. And the woods around my parents' former home are gradually being cleared for cattle pastures, which in turn will no doubt give way one day to subdivisions. If you go to the woods in America in order to drive life into a corner today, you better plan on doing it in company with dirt bikes and golfers.

In fact, if, like Thoreau, you're interested in fronting the essential facts of life, you're better off going to a nursing home instead of the woods. Be forewarned, however, that it may be you who gets driven into a corner.

My mother has been my Walden Pond. Thoreau invested two years of his life in the woods there. I spent five with my mother. Following his example, I am trying to put down on these last pages what I learned at my post. Thoreau said, somewhat jauntily, that he left the woods because he "had several more lives to live and could not spare any more time for that one." But then he was a young man, barely thirty when he left

Walden and had no idea just how short a time he had left for other lives. I felt the same way at his age.

Did I enjoy making this descent into hell with my mother? No. Am I glad I did? Absolutely. And more. Grateful.

I feel as if I've been to one of those outdoor adventure camps in the Wyoming Rockies where they toughen you up for climbing cliff faces with only brogans and sunscreen for protection.

As I watched at my mother's bedside during those last days, I didn't worry so much about the ultimate destination of either her physical atoms or her future state as a synapse in the mind of God. Even Damasio's research into human consciousnesss could not clarify those matters. Instead, I wondered, what is she now? Where is she now? The she that was gone so absolutely from my own perception. I didn't know the answers to those questions either, but as long as she had had a body, whether or not she had a conscious mind, that body had showed me my duty, guided me toward what love demands.

If you are presently at that early point where I was five years ago, overwhelmed by the task ahead, you may feel like the world has been turned inside out and shaken empty. Gravity may not seem trustworthy any longer, and you may feel as if you could at any moment fall off the earth. Try to remember in those moments, even as you lie clinging to the carpet, that you are indeed driving life into a corner, which is an incredible act of courage.

Knowing my own desperation while I tried to help my parents during those years, I feel obliged at this point to gather a few nuggets that are a bit more practical and may answer more immediate needs.

1. Even the most conscientious and self-reliant of parents can grow ill or infirm, becoming dependent on a child. Indeed, the more independent the parent is, the harder it is for the family and friends to believe in the parent's uncharacteristic incapacity.

2. The parent's need for help can happen gradually or overnight. The more gradual the decline, the easier it is to ignore or deny. Setting up specific markers for estimating abilities, such

as balancing checkbooks or remembering medications, can help the incipient caregiver judge the parent's need for aid with some degree of realism.

3. Parents may not realize, may ignore, or may deny their new neediness. If they are aware of it, they may well be embarrassed, even humiliated by their situation.

4. Nevertheless, once parents begin receiving help, they will expect that assistance to continue as naturally as they expect to breathe oxygen. And they will be generally just as minimally conscious of the help as they are of oxygen.

5. However, the parent will often feel her freedom being taken from her, and almost surely get angry with this child at times.

6. This child (who are we kidding?—it's you) will get angry with the parent. For no longer being independent and invulnerable, the way mothers and fathers ought to be. And then for not being properly grateful for the care you provide.

7. The parent will not want to hear or know about any illness or difficulties you are having, any more than a small child wants to think about its parents being vulnerable.

8. You cannot follow even the ones you love best into their darkness. Nor should you. Letting yourself be sucked into their fear will only lessen your ability to help them.

9. Friends and relatives may offer their sturdy support, but they cannot bear your pain for you. Not your friends, not your own children, not even your spouse. It is both unrealistic and unfair to expect it of them.

10. When they offer their help or comfort or companionship in your grief, accept it gratefully, but remember that their lives are distinct from yours. Which is as it should be.

11. The only one you can always rely on to listen to you and understand is the Spirit of God.

12. And sometimes you're mad at him.

13. You will worry about the crosscurrents of your feelings, especially the constant conflict between anger and guilt. Plenty of people will tell you not to worry, especially about guilt. I'm not sure they're right. Even this anxiety seems to be part of the

experience. The truth is, you will worry your conflicting emotions like a dog gnawing a bone, regardless of what I or anyone else tells you.

14. I suspect, however, that you're safer being frustrated and angry with God than with your aging parents. He's used to it; he can handle it. So yell at him, not them.

15. Having someone to yell at is only one of the advantages of being aware of God at this time. I frankly do not see how people make it through experiences like this without a sense of some sustaining grace upholding them.

(Undeniably, there are stoics—I have known some myself—who do. I just don't understand how they manage to get out of bed in the morning. Having to generate on a daily basis one's own strength or even common sense out of nothing but sheer desperation and determination wears a person out. It disables you from taking in all the rest of life. It becomes harder to remember why or how you loved the person you're caring for in the first place, or why their failing flesh should be reverenced. All your energy goes into the utter drudgery of the thing. The person in the bed or the wheelchair more than anything needs to know she is not alone, that you are with her, still loving her. And you likewise need to know that someone, even if unseen, realizes what you're undergoing and will stick with you. You can go it alone if you want to, but I don't really see the point.)

16. And lastly I offer one of the best pieces of advice I have gotten during this time: Don't make it worse than it needs to be. Take care not to savor your pain. When you have a good day, tell everyone. Concentrate on watching out for any gift, however small and from whatever improbable place that it might fall in your lap, from a convenient parking place to the use of a friend's Colorado condo for a respite week. Don't let fleeting moments of pleasure go unpraised. And when there's no pleasure, be glad of the flinty truth of pain that lets you know that, like Thoreau, you are fronting the essential facts of life.

Caring for my mother has, as you might expect, changed both my perception of my own aging body and the rounding off of my life. I accept my aches and pains with better grace these days, knowing how hard my body has worked to do its job, uphold its end of the bargain. I realize now that however well I look after it, it's still going to break down, first in one place, then another. I'm no longer impatient with it when it does, though, nor as frenetic as I used to be about staving off its losses. Joints, lymph nodes, retinas, I'm grateful they've carried me so far, filtered my juices, filled me with light.

Thinking about how I want to spend my remaining life, I appreciate the literalness of that verb "spend" as my capital dwindles and depreciates. Spend it doing what? Being how?

The answers to those questions come from a different place now than they would have five years ago. Accomplishments that used to be enormously important simply seem a lot of trouble now. I obsess over fewer things. Maybe my answers simply come from my metabolism now. That's fine by me. At this point, I have a lot of respect for metabolism.

At the same time, I feel more kindly disposed than ever to younger people, so intent on building careers, families, muscles. They are lovely in their intensity. Watching them, I see again how it feels to have life spread out before you like a feast. Only a pinched sort of soul wouldn't hunger for that feast. But having satisfied that hunger, I'm clearing my palate for some other and heretofore unknown taste.

Whenever it occurs to me that I won't be around for, say, peace in the Middle East or the first flight to Mars, I don't find that a disturbing or even startling notion. Those scenes will belong to other actors, and I'm happy to leave it to them.

I watched a doctor on television last week explain how, after being diagnosed with terminal lung cancer, he decided to reject chemotherapy. He knew it might buy him a little more time, but he also knew how miserable the treatment would make his remaining days. Later, however, he did allow radiation for a tumor in his spine, not in order to prolong his life but so that he could remain mobile as long as possible. This decision struck me as eminently sensible. I hope to use the same strategy in my own skirmishes with disease and decline, researching, weighing gains against losses, deciding what to treat and what to let go.

I think a lot about getting old and dying these days. When I was a lot younger my thoughts of death tended toward either the romantic or the speculative. In my twenties I read with enjoyable melancholy Keats's sonnet, "When I have fears that I may cease to be / before my pen has glean'd my teeming brain," and imagined my own lamented demise. Keats earned those lines by actually dying at twenty-six, while I, on the other hand, have been fruitful and multiplied.

In another youthful mood, I praised Dylan Thomas's injunction to his father to not "go gentle into that good night," but instead to "rage, rage against the dying of the light." That seemed properly Promethean to me at twenty and even thirty. But no more. People my age may imagine themselves Sisyphus, but not Prometheus. We're more likely to feel as if we've been rolling a boulder up a hill than that we're up to stealing fire from the gods.

Nevertheless, I have not yet given up my image of death as the Great Voyage Out, though, as I've said, I have downgraded my expectations about the kind of craft I'll set sail in. Rather than setting sail, my mother simply drifted out to sea, cut loose from her moorings.

As for my own outward voyage, I feel as though it's time, if not to start packing for that journey, then to start the washing and mending that has to be done beforehand.

From watching my mother's decline, I know that, before I set out, I may lose not only my body but my mind. And possibly, in the chasm that can open between those two components, even my self—though I'm not entirely convinced of that.

Though toward the end, my mother lived in a perpetual semi-dream state, unable to articulate a thought or to communicate except by gesture or look, even then something essential remained of her self. I was there, it occurred to me, if for no other reason, to recognize that self, to say yes, this is my mother.

I wanted to be able to comfort her with the knowledge that, even in her last suffering, she continued to teach me. What she had feared would be a burden has turned into a boon. Where else but at her bedside have I learned, as the psalmist put it, "to number our days that we may apply our hearts unto wisdom"?

She made possible the provisioning of my little coracle for what could be a particularly rough passage. Practical work, the sort she could take particular delight in knowing she'd done. It is her suffering that has shown me how my mind, and perhaps even my very self, may be taken from me by disease or deterioration. So I hope to apply my heart unto the wisdom of handing myself over, consigning it, returning it, with grateful thanks, to its source.

Such a job I can contemplate almost with joy and certainly with curiosity. And, since learning that wisdom could easily fill the rest of the time I have left, I should begin now. My desire to apply my heart to this task, my confidence to undertake it, comes from her mothering—an advantage that, orphan as she was, she never knew.

When a friend asked Leon Wieseltier why he was saying Kaddish for his father—a man with whom, one suspects, Wieseltier had "unresolved issues"—he answered, "Because it is my duty to my father. Because it is my duty to my religion. These are the strong reasons, the non-utilitarian, non-therapeutic reasons. Because it would be harder for me not to say Kaddish. I would despise myself. Because the fulfillment of my duty leaves my thoughts about my father unimpeded by regret and undistorted by guilt."

If the past is important to us at all, if we would preserve our memory of the people we love and who yet will surely die, we must take care not to muddy those waters. Duty clears the water.

After my mother died, I didn't want night voices lurking in the corners of my mind, darkening my days. Like Wieseltier, I want my thoughts about my mother unimpeded by regret and undistorted by guilt. And, like Wieseltier, I find the contemporary version of grief therapy too utilitarian to do us much good. He believes that in its stead we need some totally impractical formalized act to observe after suffering a great loss, some ritual. "For therapy to be effective," he says, "it must be impractical. It must refer to the ideal." Which is why he took up saying Kaddish for his father.

This prayer (named with the Aramaic version of the Hebrew word for "holy") makes no mention of the dead whatsoever. Consisting of only a few words that hallow God's name, it is routinely used in synagogue to close a section of the service. The tradition obliging sons to "say Kaddish" for their fathers began in the Middle Ages. It is not an act of private piety one can undertake in the comfort of one's own home. The son must participate in the synagogue prayer service—which itself requires a minyan, a quorum of at least ten men—every day for a year.

Taking on what appeared to outsiders a ridiculous task sometimes struck Wieseltier as absurd, especially during those times when he was away from home and had to find a minyan in unfamiliar territory so he could fulfill his commitment. Yet the very impracticality, the rational senselessness of the act was, at least in part, the point. He had to, as it were, put himself out. In this case, out of the house.

Prayer, especially for a Protestant like me, is often too mental, a function of the brain alone, or, scarcely better, the heart alone. But Wieseltier compares learning to pray with learning to dance. By arduous practice, the dancer absorbs the steps into his body so that he need no longer think about the movement. "Thinking of tradition is not the same thing as doing something with tradition," he says. Enacting ritual with the body points beyond itself. "The highest object of study is not study. The highest object of movement is not movement. The highest object of Judaism is not Judaism."

What the highest object is, Wieseltier never says. I don't fault him for this; after all, he's only just gotten close enough to the faith of his father, after decades of irritation, to dance with it again.

Thomas Lynch, a Catholic poet who wrote *The Undertaking: Life Studies from the Dismal Trade* about his day job as a mortician, has his own take on the urgency of last rites. He describes an altercation between one of his customers, a mother whose daughter had just died of leukemia, and an Episcopal deacon who advised the woman not to worry about the sorry appearance of her dead daughter. After all, the deacon told her, the body was "just a shell."

The mother smacked him a good one, Lynch reports, obviously sharing her indignation. The deacon might as well have said the dead girl with her bald head was having "a bad hair day . . . or that our hope for heaven on her behalf was based on the belief that Christ raised *just* a body from death. What if, rather than crucifixion, he'd opted for suffering low self-esteem for the remission of sins? What if rather than just a shell he'd raised his personality, say, or the idea of himself? Do you think they'd have changed the calendar for that? Done the crusades? Burned witches? Easter was a body-and-blood thing. No symbol, no euphemism, no half measure."

Until I encountered Lynch, I had been toying with the notion of cremation. It's so portable, so tidy, and relatively inexpensive. But for Lynch, efficiency isn't the point. Like Wieseltier, he believes in being impractical about death. The living need the visible reminder of death. Opting for mere convenience diminishes the honor we do the dead. Such a ceremony ought to be an effort, take up time, disrupt our lives.

Here in Texas, we used to see funeral corteges winding their way sedately through town, sometimes to country graveyards miles outside the city limits. The driving citizenry pulled over to the side of the road and waited, heads uncovered, as the solemn procession passed by. It gave us all the time and occasion to contemplate mortality. One rarely sees the sight any more. We're poorer for its disappearance.

Between them, my two daughters now have six children. Through our three generations of bodies runs a literal string of messages, etched in that most elegant of scripts, deoxyribonucleic acid. This chain, ladder, stream of life—call it by whatever metaphor you like—carries the letters of the dead to the yet-unborn. What are they saying? What do I want my own note, tacked to the string, to say?

Only this: Loving people is such a burden. If love, in and of itself, weren't the center from which life flows, if it didn't, as Dante says, move the stars, how could we bear such weight? Nevertheless, love is also all that endures. Like most of God's work, it is double-bladed. Its seed grafted into us, it may begin as an instinct, but in the end, love is a choice. As for free creatures, it must be. It is indistinguishable from choosing life.

To all those babies yet unborn who will carry her special script in their cells, the children my mother brooded over like the Holy Ghost, I send the truest words I know and that she lived: Take up the burden, embrace the blessing, move the stars.